The Teacher's Survival Guide

How Unhealed Trauma Shapes Teaching, Leadership, and School Culture

Ingrid Fullerton

NJ Learning for All, LLC

Why This Guide Exists

This guide is not an argument for leaving the classroom. It is not a call to walk away.

It is an invitation for awareness. My goal is to equip teachers with the knowledge, language, and tools they were never formally given. No educator should feel trapped in an environment that slowly erodes their well-being simply because they believe all schools are the same. In fact even within a district, there are variation in teacher's experience.

Schools differ not only in leadership style, but also in emotional culture, psychological safety, and how teachers are treated when challenges arise. Teachers deserve professional environments that align not only with their credentials and skill sets, but also with their emotional needs, values, and capacity to sustain the demands of the role. In many cases, however, educators do not fully understand the true nature of a school environment until after they have signed a contract and begun working within the system.

By that point, many teachers feel compelled to remain, even when the environment is not a healthy fit. Leaving early in one's tenure is often viewed negatively, and educators may worry that doing so will reflect poorly on their professionalism or commitment. As a result, some endure conditions that lead to burnout, emotional strain, and diminished effectiveness in the classroom.

This mindset must shift. It should be professionally acceptable for educators to recognize when a school environment does not align with their strengths, values, or well-being and to make the decision to transition without stigma. In fact, there is professional integrity in acknowledging one's limits and choosing to step away, rather than remaining in a setting where prolonged stress may affect both the teacher and their students.

Recognizing my own limitations allowed me to understand that not being a strong fit within a particular school district was not a reflection of weakness, but an important act of professional self-awareness. Rather than internalizing misalignment as failure, I chose to continue searching with purpose.

Each district I worked in contributed to my development as an educator. None of those experiences were wasted. Even when a setting was not the right long-term fit, it offered lessons, perspective, and opportunities for growth. The teacher I am today is directly shaped by the principals and leaders I have worked alongside.

Each environment, each challenge, and each transition provided a chance to refine my practice, strengthen my resilience, and deepen my understanding of what effective teaching requires.

Through time, reflection, and discernment, I eventually found a school where I could teach with integrity, stability, and joy, an environment where dignity is preserved, professional growth is encouraged, and support is authentic. What I discovered is not rare; however, it does require educators to believe that such environments exist and to trust themselves enough to seek them.

If you find yourself crying in the bathroom during your prep period or sitting in your car before school trying to pull yourself together, this book is for you.

COPYRIGHT PAGE

This book is a work of nonfiction based on lived experience, research, and professional insight.

This book is not intended to replace professional mental health and medical advice. Readers are encouraged to seek qualified professionals for individualized support.

Published by
NJ Learning for All, LLC

Printed in the United States of America

ISBN: 979-8-9930033-2-0

NJlearningforall@gmail.com

Table of Contents

Chapter 1 — Not All Trauma Leaves Bruises
When the Classroom Activates What No One Sees........................9

Chapter 2 —Why So Many Teachers Are Drawn to Education
When Teaching Isn't an Accident...16

Chapter 3—How Childhood Adaptations Shape Professional Processing, Supervision, and Teacher Well-Being
From Childhood Survival to Professional Response.......................20

Chapter 4 —A Common Instructional Moment
When Depth Is Misread...23

Chapter 5 — The Cost of Integrity: When Justice Is Misread
A Reflection on Autistic Traits in Educators..................................30

Chapter 6 — When Authority Masks Unhealed Trauma
The Hidden Line Between Support and Exploitation....................36

Chapter 7 — School: The Perfect Storm
How the Residue of Abuse in Children Shows Up in the Classroom...43

Chapter 8 — When Teachers and Staffs Activate Children's Wounds
Why Power Struggles Escalate Instead of Resolve..........................49

Chapter 9 — How Nervous Systems Respond to Disrespect in the Classroom
Regulation, Authority, and the Moment of Choice........................55

Chapter 10 — Trust-Building With Students Who Resist Adults
Safety, Regulation, and the Psychology of Real Learning...............61

Chapter 11 — Where Classroom and Family Realities Meet
Understanding the Parent Side of the Conversation.......................70

Chapter 12 — The Influence Teachers Already Hold
When Parents Don't Respond the Way, We Expect.......................76

Chapter 13 — When Responsibility Feels Dangerous
Discipline, Fear, and Parental Helplessness.....................................79

Chapter 14 — Navigating Challenging Parents While Staying Professional
When a Parent Believes the Child First...84

Chapter 15 — When Adult Workplace Dynamics Mirror Adolescence
When Integrity Meets Insecurity in School Communities.............91

Chapter 16 — For the Teacher Who Feels Threatened by a Colleague's Success
Understanding What You Can't See, Yet..98

Chapter 17 —When Trauma Comes From Above
How Administrators Can Activate Wounds in Teachers............109

Chapter 18 How an Administrator Can Feel Threatened by a Teacher
(Without the Teacher Intending Harm) 115

Chapter 19 How Unresolved Trauma Shapes Conflict Between Teachers and Leadership
When Trauma Meets Trauma..120

Chapter 20 When One Leader Changes Everything
How a Single Traumatic Experience Can Alter a Teacher's Sense of Safety..123

Chapter 21 When the Body Knows Before the Mind
How Trauma Lives in Teachers Long After the Bell Rings.........127

Chapter 22 How Unhealed Wounds Distort Professional Judgment
Unhealed wounds do not stay contained.......................................131

Chapter 23 What Teachers Need From Leadership
Why Regulated Administrators Create Motivated Schools..........136

Chapter 24 Is This Happening Now or Is This Memory?
Teaching the Nervous System to Tell the Difference..................143

Chapter 25 Protecting Yourself While You Teach
Practical Tools for Staying Regulated, Grounded, and Whole....149

Chapter 26 Understanding the System: The Game Behind the Profession
How to Navigate Professional Dynamics Without Losing Your Integrity..156

Chapter 27
Your Integrity as a Teacher Still Matters
Choosing Dignity and Strength in a Profession That Tests Both..165

Dedication

This book is dedicated

To my husband,

whose love, patience, encouragement, and unwavering support carried me through late nights grading papers, creating lesson plans, and researching frameworks and standards. I am proud and honored to call you my husband.

To my daughters,

you rarely complained during the moments when you needed me but the demands of my work as a teacher limited my ability to be present. Your love has been my anchor. I know that God loves me because I am blessed with the most compassionate, loving, appreciative daughters. You often makes me believe that I was enough at times that I felt that you deserved more. Thank you!

To the principal,

who recognized my strengths and was not afraid to acknowledge them. You never treated my shortcomings as something to punish. Instead, you led with encouragement, patience, and example. Having worked with many principals throughout my career, I can say with confidence that your leadership is rare. It is grounded in integrity, guided by compassion, and powerful in its ability to inspire teachers to believe in themselves.

.

And to the teachers,

who reminded me that a true professional community still exists, a place where educators support one another despite the negativity surrounding our profession, where there is no competition, only the shared belief that when one teacher succeeds, we all succeed.

Chapter 1

Not All Trauma Leaves Bruises

When the Classroom Activates What No One Sees

Teaching has never been a simple profession. It has always required patience, emotional strength, and the ability to lead young minds through uncertainty. But in today's educational climate, the weight placed on teachers has grown far beyond instruction. Teachers are now expected to be educators, counselors, mediators, and behavioral specialists.

Across the country, regardless of state, district, or grade level, teachers are leaving the profession at an alarming rates. The national teacher shortage is no longer a projection; it is a reality unfolding in real time. The question is no longer why teachers are struggling? The question has become how much more they can carry before they are forced to walk away?

Teachers are working in environments where expectations increase while authority narrows. Schools operate under intense scrutiny, and disciplinary decisions that are no longer simple. Just as many parents now hesitate to discipline their own children out of fear of judgment or legal consequences, school administrators experience a parallel pressure. Funding and accountability metrics are often tied to disciplinary data, and attendance.

At the same time, classrooms have become more emotionally charged. Students arrive carrying stress, trauma, anxiety, and unmet needs. Teachers are expected to respond calmly, professionally, and compassionately even when they are confronted with disrespect, defiance, or personal insults.

This is the reality: teachers absorb emotional impact every day while being expected to remain composed.

Now imagine carrying all of that responsibility while also carrying unhealed childhood trauma.

This book begins with one essential truth: teachers do not leave education only because of workload, policy, or pay.
Many leave because of the emotional weight they carry silently.

When people hear the word trauma, many imagine extreme or visible harm.
Bruises.
Broken bones.
Police reports.
Court records.
Events that clearly cross a line.
But trauma is not defined by how dramatic an experience looks from the outside.
It is defined by how unsafe, alone, or overwhelmed a child felt while it was happening.

Adverse Childhood Experiences, commonly called ACEs are experiences that occur during childhood and shape how a person learns to cope with stress, relationships, authority, and responsibility. Some ACEs are obvious. Others are quiet, normalized, and rarely named.

This chapter divides ACEs into two broader groupings, not to compare wounds, but to deepen awareness and help more readers recognize their own story within these pages.

The Obvious Forms Adverse Childhood Experiences

Physical abuse
Direct harm to a child's body by an adult or caregiver.
Examples include:
• Being hit, slapped, shaken, or restrained

• Being injured as punishment
• Living with fear of physical harm

Sexual abuse or exploitation
Any sexual violation involving a child.
Examples include:
• Unwanted sexual contact
• Exposure to sexual material or behavior
• Sexual coercion by an adult or older child

Severe emotional abuse
Repeated verbal or psychological harm.
Examples include:
• Constant humiliation or belittling
• Threats, intimidation, or emotional cruelty
• Being told you are worthless, bad, or unwanted

Domestic violence
Exposure to violence or threats between adults in the home.
Examples include:
• Witnessing physical fights
• Hearing threats or destruction of property
• Living in constant fear of escalation

Severe neglect
Failure to meet a child's basic physical needs.

Examples include:
• Lack of food, hygiene, or medical care
• Being left unsupervised for long periods
• Unsafe or unstable living conditions

Caregiver substance abuse
Living with an adult whose substance use created instability or fear.

Examples include:
• Unpredictable behavior due to alcohol or drugs
• A child assuming adult responsibilities
• Fear of the caregiver's mood or actions

Untreated severe mental illness in the home
Caregiver mental health struggles that affected safety or consistency.
Examples include:
• Emotional withdrawal or unpredictability
• Episodes that frightened the child
• Lack of explanation or reassurance

Incarceration of a parent or caregiver
Sudden and often confusing separation from a caregiver.
Examples include:
• Loss of daily contact with a parent
• Stigma or secrecy surrounding the absence
• Lack of emotional support during the separation

These experiences are widely recognized as traumatic. Many people who lived through them know something harmful occurred even if they struggle to speak about it.

The Less Obvious Forms of Adverse Childhood Experiences

Emotional neglect
A lack of emotional support, comfort, or responsiveness.
Examples include:
• Feelings being ignored or minimized
• Being told to "stop crying" instead of being comforted
• Having no one notice emotional distress

Chronic emotional distance

Caregivers who were physically present but emotionally unavailable.

Examples include:

- Limited affection or warmth
- Little interest in the child's inner world
- Emotional needs consistently unmet

Parentification

A child taking on adult emotional or caregiving roles.

Examples include:

- Managing a parent's emotions
- Caring for siblings beyond age-appropriate expectations
- Being relied on for adult concerns

High-conflict home without physical violence

Ongoing emotional tension or hostility.

Examples include:

- Frequent arguments
- Walking on eggshells
- Constant emotional strain in the household

Parental separation or divorce

When separation resulted in instability or emotional harm.

Examples include:

- Being placed in the middle of adult conflict
- Loss of emotional support
- Sudden changes in routines or caregivers

Inconsistent caregiving

Unpredictable expectations, rules, or support.

Examples include:

- Shifting standards of behavior

• Caregivers who were warm one moment and withdrawn the next
• Uncertainty about what was expected

Lack of protection or advocacy
Adults failing to intervene when harm occurred.
Examples include:
• Bullying being dismissed
• Abuse or distress minimized
• Learning that asking for help was ineffective

Excessive responsibility at a young age
A child being relied on too early.
Examples include:
• Managing household tasks beyond age level
• Being "the strong one"
• Feeling responsible for others' well-being

Conditional love or approval
Love depends on behavior or achievement.
Examples include:
• Praise only when compliant or successful
• Withdrawal of affection as punishment
• Feeling valued for performance, not presence

Chronic invalidation
Repeated dismissal of a child's inner experience.
Examples include:
• Being told feelings were wrong or exaggerated
• Being labeled "too sensitive"
• Learning not to trust one's own emotions

Many people with these experiences say:
"Nothing bad really happened."
"Other people had it worse."
"My parents did the best they could."

All of those statements can be true, but often the nervous system don't believe it.
And the impact can still be real.

Children adapt to the environments they grow up in, learning to stay quiet, be helpful, remain in control, closely read others, and avoid needing too much in order to survive.

These adaptations often become strengths. But adaptation is not the same as safety.

Some wounds are loud.
Some are quiet.
Both shape how adults respond to stress, authority, and responsibility.

Chapter 2

Why So Many Teachers Are Drawn to Education

When Teaching Isn't an Accident

For many teachers, the pull toward education isn't random. It isn't just a love of content, or a talent for explaining things. For some, teaching is the first-place life starts to feel organized, predictable, and emotionally safer than what came before.

Psychology has long recognized a pattern in which individuals are drawn to helping roles in part because of their own lived pain. In this text, I refer to this pattern as the nervous-system translator, a person who transforms early adaptation into connection and purpose through helping.

And when you look at the data, you can see why this resonates with so many educators.

In a study of early care and education teachers, 72.9% reported at least one ACE, and 22.2% reported four or more.

Those numbers don't "prove" why someone became a teacher. But they do support the point that a large share of educators are carrying childhood adversity into adulthood often quietly.

Adverse Childhood Experiences and the Need to Finally Be in Control

One of the most common long-term effects of childhood adversity is this: the body learns that safety depends on what can be predicted, managed, or prevented. That is why control becomes so appealing, not as arrogance, but as protection. Research on trauma and stress consistently points to perceived control as a major factor in how people respond to threatening or painful experiences. When control feels absent, distress tends to rise; when control feels possible, the nervous system can settle.

Teaching offers a powerful illusion, and at times a genuine experience, of control. It brings structure through routines, schedules, rules, and lesson plans that create order. It offers a role with purpose being the steady adult, creating predictability for others, and watching growth emerge from what was carefully built.

It also provides a clear identity: I am the teacher. I know what to do. I can help. For someone whose childhood felt chaotic, unsafe, or emotionally unpredictable, education can become the first environment where they finally feel, I have a say. I can lead. I can create stability.

Why Students Can Feel Non-Threatening to Teachers With Adverse Childhood Experiences

This distinction helps explain a familiar refrain among educators who leave the teaching profession: they rarely say they left because of students; they say they left because of the adults.

While students can be demanding, they do not control employment, evaluate professional worth, or have power over institutional authority. For individuals with histories of adversity, early harm was often associated with adults who held power over safety, approval, or survival.

As a result, the nervous system may remain particularly sensitive to adult power dynamics. When school environments replicate these dynamics through evaluation, surveillance, or punitive leadership, the body responds with threat, not reflection. In this way, teacher attrition is often less about the classroom and more about the conditions created by adult authority.

School can feel like the "safe world" once remembered

Many educators with Adversity histories remember school as more stable than home, a place with routines, predictable adults, and clear expectations. So education becomes a way of returning to the only environment that once felt anchored.

This doesn't mean every teacher with ACEs sees students this way.
It means for many, the classroom becomes the first place where closeness feels possible without the same threat level.

The Hidden Risk: When Service Becomes a Search for Repair

Some educators aren't only teaching children.
They are also, without realizing it, trying to rewrite something they never got.

That's the heart of the nervous system translator dynamic: lived pain can produce empathy and skill, but it can also produce unconscious missions.

For many ACE survivors, teaching feels like a place where protection is finally possible. When someone grows up without reliable protection, they often become highly attentive to other people's emotions and quick to notice signs that someone might be hurting. In a classroom, that sensitivity can feel like a strength. It can look like stepping in when a child is being left out, reading tension before it escalates, or noticing a student's sadness before anyone else does.

Even normal school moments like a disagreement between peers can trigger a strong protective response. Not because the teacher doesn't understand that conflict is part of childhood, but because their instincts are trained to prevent emotional harm.

For someone who learned early that pain could be ignored or minimized, the idea of "waiting to see what happens" can feel risky. Teaching offers a role where intervention is allowed, caring is expected, and safety can be created in real time.

That is one reason many ACE survivors are drawn to education; the classroom becomes a place where they can give what they once needed, an adult who notices, steps in, and protects.

What This Means for Teachers

This chapter is not here to diagnose educators.
It's here to explain a reality:

When you have ACEs, you may enter education because it offers what childhood did not:

- structure
- purpose
- identity
- authority without cruelty
- control without chaos

And when that motivation is understood, teaching becomes safer, not only for students, but for the teacher.

Chapter 3

How Childhood Adaptations Shape Professional Processing, Supervision, and Teacher Well-Being

From Childhood Survival to Professional Response

Teaching does not begin in the classroom.
It begins in the nervous system.

Long before a lesson is written, long before a standard is posted on the board, a teacher's body is already interpreting the world, authority, feedback, tone, power, approval.

In earlier chapters, we explored why many educators are drawn to education. For some, the classroom offers structure, identity, predictability, and a sense of protective authority that childhood did not always provide.

But what happens when the very adaptations that helped someone survive childhood begin shaping how they process feedback, authority, and professional tension?

This chapter explores how unexamined childhood adaptations show up in everyday professional experiences, especially during supervision and evaluation.

Because trauma does not only shape behavior.
It shapes perception.
It shapes interpretation.
It shapes reaction.

Unless we understand that, we may misinterpret our own responses.

The Adaptations That Become Teaching Strengths

Children adapt in order to survive.

A child who grows up in unpredictability may become highly attuned to emotional shifts.
A child who grows up in chaos may become structured and organized.
A child who feels unheard may become articulate and precise.
A child who lacked protection may become fiercely protective.

What began as survival often becomes strength.

In teaching, those adaptations look like:

- attentiveness to student emotion
- commitment to fairness
- high standards
- deep preparation

The very traits that make someone an effective educator may have originated as protective strategies.

But protective strategies do not disappear when the environment changes.
They follow us.

When Adaptation Meets Professional Authority

School systems contain hierarchy.

Hierarchy simply means that authority is structured in levels. Some roles hold decision-making power over other roles. In most districts, the superintendent oversees principals, principals oversee supervisors and teachers, supervisors oversee curriculum implementation, and teachers implement instruction with students.

Each level has defined responsibilities and authority. Decisions typically flow downward, while feedback flows upward in more limited ways. Understanding hierarchy is not about agreeing with every decision; it is about recognizing where power sits, who has the final say, and how influence moves within the system.

For many teachers, these are simply professional structures.

For others with histories of adversity, these structures can awaken something older.

Because early trauma often involved:

- adults with power
- unpredictable authority
- approval tied to performance
- correction without explanation
- rules that shifted without warning

When modern professional authority mirrors even a small piece of those early dynamics, the nervous system reacts, not just to the present moment, but to accumulated memory.

This does not mean the administrator is harmful.

It means the body is sensitive to power.

And power, especially when attached to evaluation, can feel personal.

Chapter 4

A Common Instructional Moment

When Depth Is Misread

A middle school mathematics teacher designs a lesson on box plots. Instead of teaching the procedure mechanically, she builds conceptual understanding using fractional reasoning. Students explore quartiles as divisions of a data set into fourths. The median is connected to halves. The structure becomes mathematically meaningful, not just something to label.

Students engage.
They explain their reasoning.
They demonstrate understanding.

During the post-observation conference, the evaluator states:

"Fractions have nothing to do with box plots."

The teacher leaves the meeting stunned. Confused. Quietly questioning.

She immediately wonders:
Does this administrator dislike me?

She struggles to reconcile the feedback with what she knows to be mathematically sound. It is difficult for her to believe that an administrator who was once a math teacher would not recognize that a quartile represents one fourth of a whole. The confusion unsettles her. Is this a knowledge gap or something else? When logic does not explain the situation, the mind searches for motive. And in the absence of clarity, self-doubt quietly begins to grow.

What she does not yet realize is this:

From a content perspective, her lesson reflected conceptual teaching.
From the supervision perspective, the feedback reflected a procedural lens.

But the deeper impact is not mathematical.

It is psychological.

It is about:

- voice
- authority
- reasoning
- being heard

When Feedback Becomes a Rating

The feedback does not end with the comment.

It ends with a **"partial effective"** rating.

And that changes everything.

A comment can be discussed but a rating becomes documentation.

In many districts, that label carries weight. It may influence:

- professional reputation
- growth plans
- future observations
- leadership opportunities
- self-confidence
- long-term career trajectory

When a teacher has invested deeply in preparation and conceptual clarity and students clearly demonstrate understanding, a partial effective rating can feel disproportionate.

The nervous system does not interpret ratings neutrally.

It interprets them as signals of safety or threat.

Am I secure here?
Am I seen accurately?
Do I need to protect myself?
The body reacts before logic can intervene.

The Psychological Impact of a Lower Rating

For teachers whose identity is tied to competence and preparation, a rating like "partial effective" can activate powerful internal narratives:

Performance labels are experienced not only as feedback about practice, but as judgments of identity.

The teacher may change schools.
Teach new students.
Grow professionally.

But the memory of that rating may remain vivid.

The body remembers moments when competence felt questioned under power.

What Professional Activation Looks Like

Activation does not always look dramatic.

It can look like:

- replaying feedback repeatedly

- urgency to clarify or defend
- tightness in the chest after meetings
- difficulty "letting something go"
- intense questioning of competence
- assuming personal fault when misalignment occurs

Externally, the teacher appears professional.

Internally, the nervous system is working to restore safety.

The Hidden Belief

Many high-functioning educators carry an unspoken rule learned early in life:

If I do things correctly, I will be safe.

In childhood, safety may have meant:

- avoiding punishment
- avoiding rejection
- avoiding emotional withdrawal

In adulthood, it becomes:

- preparing thoroughly
- anticipating needs
- preventing mistakes
- performing well

So when feedback feels unclear or misaligned, the internal alarm sounds:

Something is wrong. Fix it.

But the body is not chasing perfection.

It is chasing safety.

Regulated vs. Unregulated Processing

An unregulated nervous system may interpret the rating as:

"I am not effective."
"I need to protect myself."
"I should minimize visibility."

A regulated nervous system pauses and separates:

The rating reflects one evaluator's lens.
The rating does not define instructional depth.
The rating does not erase student understanding.

Regulation creates space between event and identity.

When activation goes unnamed, teachers assume the problem is themselves.

Understanding processing is not self-indulgence.

It is professional sustainability.

The Message the Teacher Needed but Never Received

The truth is this: the teacher was doing what strong teachers do. She was connecting ideas, protecting student understanding, and refusing to let learning become mechanical.

What she experienced was not a failure of teaching.
It was a moment when her depth was not met with depth from her administrator.

And that mismatch hurts more than people realize.

Because for many educators, teaching is not simply a job. It is an extension of how they think, how they prepare, and how seriously they take their responsibility to students. When their thinking is reduced, dismissed, or misunderstood, it does not feel procedural. It feels personal.

What she needed in that moment was simple and direct acknowledgment:

“I see what you were doing.
I understand why you chose that approach.
Your reasoning makes sense.
Your students benefited from it.
Even if adjustments are necessary, your depth is not a liability.”

Instead, she was left alone to interpret the interaction.

And slowly, a question formed that no teacher should have to carry:

Is my strength a problem here?

Without clarity, strong educators often turn inward. They replay conversations. They dissect their tone. They question their judgment. They search for error where there may have only been misalignment.

But the message she should have received was this:

Her thinking was not the problem.
Her preparation was not the problem.
Her commitment to deep understanding was not the problem.
She was intentional.

And intentional teachers are the ones who transform how students experience learning.

One evaluator's lens does not define intelligence.
One rating does not erase impact.
One moment does not rewrite professional identity.

Many teachers have walked out of observations carrying more weight than guidance. Many have absorbed silence as criticism. Many have internalized ambiguity as failure.

And feeling the impact years later does not make her fragile. It makes her human.

The part of her that felt wounded was the same part that cares deeply about doing this work well.

That part should not be silenced.

It should be protected.

Because that is the part that makes students feel seen.
That is the part that refuses to reduce learning to compliance.
That is the part that remains committed to understanding.

And that part is not a liability.

It is her strength.

Chapter 5

The Cost of Integrity: When Justice Is Misread

A Reflection on Autistic Traits in Educators

There is a population of educators rarely named in professional discourse.

They are not disruptive.
They are not incompetent.
They are not disloyal.

They are deeply anchored in integrity.
And sometimes, neurologically different.

I write this chapter not as an outside observer, but as someone who lives with many of the traits associated with autism, particularly heightened sensitivity, a deep internal code of justice, and an unwavering commitment to integrity.

For years, I did not have a language for it.

I only knew that I experienced the professional world differently from most teachers.

And for a long time, I carried shame because of that difference. Shame for being misunderstood in spaces where my only intention was to serve my students with honesty and integrity.

Living With an Internal Code

If something feels unjust, it registers in my nervous system immediately.

Justice is not a preference for me.
It is an internal requirement, one I sometimes find difficult to

ignore, especially when it involves children. Resisting it can feel as unnatural as trying not to breathe when oxygen is present.

For years, I struggled to understand why this part of me was not always recognized as a strength, and why I was so often misunderstood. Questions I asked for clarification were interpreted as stubbornness. My intent was never to challenge authority, but to better understand the direction so I could align my actions with expectations.

It was not until I began to recognize my own autistic traits that these experiences started to make sense.

The very things people once interpreted as annoying, my need for clarity, my directness, my sensitivity to fairness, were the same traits that shaped my strengths as an educator.

They were not deficits.
They were part of my neurological makeup.

They were, in many ways, my professional superpower.

And I hope this chapter reaches teachers who have quietly asked themselves the same question I once asked:

Why am I always misunderstood when I am trying so hard to do right thing?

When an educator consistently speaks about justice, people begin to associate them with defiance.
When an educator does not participate in gossip or politics, they may be perceived as unapproachable.

If you are autistic or carry strong autistic traits, your communication may be:

direct rather than socially buffered
integrity-driven rather than strategic
transparent rather than performative

In hierarchical systems, this can be misunderstood.

People often project motive onto request for clarity.

When Integrity Becomes a Liability

In misaligned schools, integrity is praised publicly.
But privately, systems often reward alignment over authenticity.
You may have been unintentionally threatening individuals who rely on ambiguity.

You may represent a personality that cannot be easily managed through social pressure.

If you have ever:

been blamed for something because you are "the outspoken one"
been excluded because your honesty made others uncomfortable
wondered why integrity seemed to create distance rather than respect

Listen very keenly:

There is nothing wrong with you.
There is nothing wrong with your commitment to fairness.
There is nothing wrong with needing truth to feel stable.

Moving Forward Without Losing Yourself

For educators who recognize themselves here, protection does not require silence. It requires support and strategy.

Continue to seek clarity rather than assume intent.
Acting against your wiring will eventually turn you against yourself.

Remain true to who you are.

It is okay to walk alone for a time.
You were made this way for a purpose you may not yet fully understand.

Continue to trust yourself.
You do not need to dilute your integrity to remain employable.

What you need is not environments where your cognitive style is understood.

School systems must begin providing intentional training for administrators on the characteristics of educators who are neurodivergent, particularly those on the autism spectrum.

Misunderstanding is not neutral.
It carries consequences.

When administrators are not trained to recognize neurodivergent traits in adults, they may misinterpret:

- Direct communication as defiance
- Clarifying questions as challenge
- Emotional regulation differences as coldness
- Precision as rigidity
- Ethical consistency as opposition

But many educators on the spectrum are among the most loyal employees a school will ever have.

They protect structure.

They value clear systems.

They follow policy faithfully.

They prepare relentlessly.

They are deeply student-centered.

They are often highly-performing and ethically consistent.

They do not destabilize culture.

They stabilize it.

They are the teachers who protect students fiercely.
They are the teachers who do not cut corners.
They are the teachers who will hold the line when standards matter.

However, they may struggle in environments where expectations are implicit, hierarchy is politically layered, and feedback is ambiguous.

It is a mismatch of operating systems.

When leaders misread integrity as insubordination, they do not simply lose a teacher's trust.

They lose a stabilizing force in the building.

They lose quiet loyalty.

This chapter is an invitation to awareness.

Neurodivergent educators are already in every building.

They are not rare.

They are often simply undiagnosed, misunderstood, or masking.

Training administrators to recognize adult neurodivergence is not accommodation. It is leadership literacy.

There are leaders who understand this.

Leaders who value clarity.
Leaders who protect integrity-driven staff.
Leaders who recognize that honesty is not insubordination.
Leaders who understand that structure and sensitivity can coexist.

Those leaders change everything.

They create schools where strong teachers do not have to shrink to survive.

If you have not found that environment yet, continue searching.

Do not abandon yourself to fit a system that refuses to understand you.

The goal is not to become smaller.

The goal is to find leadership that recognizes your strength.

Chapter 6

When Authority Masks Unhealed Trauma

The Hidden Line Between Support and Exploitation

Unhealed trauma does not vanish when an adult gains responsibility over others. In fact, authority can mask it, rationalize it, and quietly feed it.

Adults who were deprived of affection, safety, or validation as children often carry a deep, unspoken hunger into adulthood. When that hunger is not acknowledged or treated, it looks for relief. For some, that relief is sought through roles that provide emotional closeness, admiration, or dependency.

Children are uniquely vulnerable in this dynamic.
They are responsive.
They seek approval.
They attach easily to adults who show interest and care.

For an adult with unresolved trauma, this responsiveness can feel profoundly regulating. What begins as "I connect well with kids" can shift into "They really need me." Then into "I'm the only one who understands them." Then into "This bond is special."

At that point, the role has changed.

The adult is no longer protecting the child.
The adult is using the child to meet unresolved emotional needs.

This is not confusion.
This is not love.
This is not help.
It is role reversal and it is abuse.

Trauma distorts perception. It convinces adults that meeting their own emotional needs through a child is nurturing rather than exploitative. Dependency is reframed as connection. Boundary erosion is reframed as trust.

A Difficult Truth That Must Be Named Clearly

Not all harm to children comes from people who see themselves as dangerous. Some harm comes from adults who sincerely believe they are helping. Which explain why so many deny causing harm to children.

When stories surface about teachers, coaches, mentors, or youth leaders who crossed boundaries, the public often asks, "How could they think this was, okay?" The answer is uncomfortable but necessary: they did not see themselves as abusers. They saw themselves as needed.

Unhealed adults often carry an internal story that sounds like this:

- No one ever showed up for me.
- I know what loneliness feels like.
- I'm giving this child what I never had.
- They trust me.
- They choose me.

But children do not choose power dynamics. They adapt to the authority and attachment structures adults create and respond to them.

These Are Signs of an Abusive Dynamic

The following patterns place a child in a role they did not choose and signal a serious risk of abuse when they appear in adults who hold authority over children. If any of these feel familiar, this is not a moment for shame,

It is a moment for honest reflection and immediate boundary correction.

An adult is moving into abusive territory when they:

- Feel most alive, valued, or emotionally regulated when a student seeks their attention
- Rely on students for comfort, validation, or emotional reassurance
- Feel distressed, jealous, or resentful when a student connects with other adults
- Resist or resent professional boundaries that limit access to students
- Create emotional "specialness," secrecy, or exclusivity
- Believe they are the only adult who truly understands or can help a child
- Justify closeness by telling themselves, "This child needs me more than others do"

These are not signs of dedication.
They are signs that the adult's needs are overpowering the teacher-student relationship.

The Line That Cannot Be Crossed

When an adult uses a child, consciously or unconsciously, for:

- Emotional regulation
- Attachment fulfillment
- A sense of worth or identity

the adult becomes the source of harm.
Even if:

- No physical boundary has been crossed
- The adult believes their intentions are pure
- The child appears attached, appreciative, or eager

Children cannot consent to being used to meet adult emotional needs.

That dynamic is abuse.

This chapter is not written to accuse teachers.
It is written to protect children and to protect adults from becoming someone they never intended to be.

If you recognize yourself anywhere in this chapter, pause.

This does not mean you are evil.
But it does mean you are at risk.

Here is the truth that must be held with absolute clarity:

When an adult depends on a child for emotional fulfillment, the adult is no longer helping.

At that moment:

- You are no longer the protector
- You are no longer the helper
- You are participating in abuse, even if it is subtle, even if it is unintentional

The ethical response is not to manage this quietly or try harder.
It is to step back, seek professional support, and remove yourself from roles that place children in emotional service of adult needs.

Accountability Is Protection

Trauma that goes unaddressed does not stay contained. When paired with authority over children, it can become exploitative, especially when emotional need is mistaken for care.

Adults are responsible for addressing their own unresolved wounds before holding power over children. Anything else places children at risk.

This chapter is not about fear.
It is about accountability.

It gives language to what many people sense but struggle to name.
It dismantles the myth that good intentions prevent harm.
And it tells the truth that:

It was never a child's role to save an adult.
Adults are responsible for healing themselves before stepping into positions of power over children.

At that point, the role has changed. The adult is no longer protecting the child; they are using the relationship to meet unresolved emotional needs. This is not confusion, love, or help. It is role reversal and it is harmful.

Trauma can distort perception. It can lead adults to believe that meeting their own emotional needs through a child is nurturing rather than exploitative. Dependency becomes reframed as connection. Boundary erosion is mistaken for trust.

A Difficult Truth That Must Be Named

Not all harm to children comes from individuals who see themselves as dangerous. Some harm comes from adults who genuinely believe they are helping, which is why denial is so common. When stories surface about teachers, coaches, mentors, or youth leaders who cross boundaries, people often ask, "How could they think this was, okay?" The uncomfortable truth is that many did not see themselves as harmful, they saw themselves as needed.

Unhealed adults may carry internal narratives such as:

- No one ever showed up for me.
- I know what loneliness feels like.
- I'm giving this child what I never had.
- They trust me.
- They choose me.

But children do not choose power dynamics. They adapt to the authority and attachment structures adults create.

Recognizing an Abusive Dynamic

When adults hold authority over children, certain patterns signal serious risk. These are not signs of dedication; they are indicators that adult needs are overtaking the teacher–student relationship.

Warning signs include:

- Feeling most emotionally regulated when a student seeks their attention
- Relying on students for comfort, validation, or reassurance
- Experiencing jealousy or distress when a student connects with other adults
- Resisting professional boundaries that limit access to students
- Creating secrecy, exclusivity, or emotional "specialness"
- Believing they are the only adult who truly understands or can help a child
- Justifying closeness by telling themselves, "This child needs me more than others do"

When a child becomes a source of emotional regulation, attachment fulfillment, or personal identity for an adult, the relationship shifts into harmful territory, even if no physical boundary has been crossed and even if intentions feel pure.

Children cannot consent to being used to meet adult emotional needs.

Accountability Protects Everyone

This chapter is not written to accuse teachers. It is written to protect children and to protect adults from becoming someone they never intended to be.

If any part of this feels familiar, it is not a moment for shame. It is a moment for reflection and boundary correction. Depending on a child for emotional fulfillment compromises the adult's role as protector and places the child at risk.

The ethical response is not to minimize the behavior or try harder within the same dynamic. It is to step back, seek professional support, and address the unresolved needs driving the attachment.

Trauma that goes unaddressed does not remain contained. When paired with authority over children, it can become exploitative, particularly when emotional need is mistaken for care. Adults are responsible for addressing their own wounds before holding power over children.

This chapter provides language for what many sense but struggle to name. It challenges the belief that good intentions alone prevent harm and affirms a critical truth:

It was never a child's role to save an adult.
Adults are responsible for their own healing before stepping into positions of power over children.

Chapter 7

School: The Perfect Storm

How the Residue of Abuse in Children Shows Up in the Classroom

Trauma in classrooms is rarely loud at first. It is more likely to appear in small moments like how someone stands, how they speak, how quickly they react. A voice changes, patience shortens, and suddenly a situation feels bigger than it should

How Trauma Shapes Student Behavior in the Classroom

Many students walk into classrooms carry Adverse Childhood Experiences (ACEs) that have trained their bodies to stay on high alert.

For these students, the classroom is not neutral.

Authority figures may feel unpredictable.
Correction may feel like rejection.
Boundaries may feel like threat.

So their bodies respond before their minds do.

What this looks like in class:

- Talking back
- Eye-rolling
- Refusal to comply
- Sudden outbursts
- Shutdown or avoidance
- Challenging authority
- Testing limits repeatedly

This is not strategic misbehavior.
It is a nervous system scanning for safety.

Students with high ACEs are often not asking:

"How did I do wrong?"

They are asking:

"Am I safe?"
"Will you abandon me?"
"Will you humiliate me?"
"Can you stay regulated when I can't?"

School is often the first place where the effects of abuse in children become visible.

Not because school causes the behavior,
but because school is where a child's suppressed fear finally has somewhere to go.

Many children who experience abuse at home do not come to school sad or withdrawn. They come in angry, defiant, aggressive, or disconnected. The fear they are forced to swallow at home has been building, and school becomes the place where it leaks out.

They may curse at teachers, challenge authority, bully other children, or get into frequent fights. Some escalate quickly when corrected. Others laugh after hurting someone or show little visible remorse.

To the outside world, this looks like bad behavior.

Psychologically, it is something else.

It is fear with nowhere to go.

Why Teachers Become the Target

Children who are abused grow up in environments where power is enforced through fear.

At home, the child has no control.
They cannot fight back.
They cannot escape.
They cannot speak freely.

School becomes the first environment where the rules change.

Teachers cannot hit them.
Authority figures are limited by policy.
Physical retaliation is not allowed.

For an abused child, this creates a powerful psychological opening.

The school becomes a place where unsafe feelings finally feel safe enough to surface.

Often without conscious awareness, the child knows that teachers cannot respond with the same level of threat they experience at home. The fear, anger, and humiliation that were never allowed to exist suddenly have a place to go, not because the teacher is weak, but because the teacher is bound by safety.

Why Remorse Is Often Missing

One of the most misunderstood signs of abuse in children is the absence of visible remorse.

Remorse requires emotional safety.
It requires empathy.
It requires the ability to slow down and reflect.

Abused children do not live in that state.

They live in constant alertness.

Their nervous systems are focused on scanning for danger, not processing emotions. When a child is operating from survival mode, the brain does not pause to think about consequences or other people's feelings. It reacts.

What adults interpret as a lack of conscience is often a frozen emotional system, one that has learned it is not safe to feel.

Bullying and Fighting as Survival Responses

Many children who bully or fight are not seeking power for enjoyment.

They are trying to regain control.

Abuse teaches a child powerful lessons:

- Power prevents pain
- Fear keeps you safe
- Weakness invites harm

So the child adapts.

By intimidating others, they feel temporarily protected.
By fighting, they release stored fear.
By dominating, they avoid being dominated.

This behavior is not random.

It is learned.

School becomes the perfect storm for abused children because of the contrast between environments.

At home:

- Emotions are suppressed

- Fear is constant
- Power is enforced through pain
- Expression is dangerous

At school:

- Adults cannot hit back
- Authority is limited
- Emotional regulation is expected

The child is asked to behave in ways they were never taught how to achieve safely.

The pressure builds.

Eventually, it explodes.

What This Feels Like for the Child

Inside the child, the experience is not anger.

It is fear.

Fear of being controlled.
Fear of being embarrassed.
Fear of being powerless.
Fear of being hurt again.

But because fear was never allowed to be expressed, it comes out misaligned.

As rage.
As defiance.
As cruelty.
As silence.

The child does not wake up wanting to hurt others.

The child wakes up trying to survive feelings they never learned how to name.

The Connection That Must Be Made

Behavior at school does not start at school.

It starts at home.

It starts in how a child is corrected.
How they are spoken to.
How fear is used.
How power is enforced.

When schools respond to abused children with punishment alone, they unknowingly repeat the same cycle that caused the harm in the first place.

Control meets control.
Fear meets fear.
And nothing changes.

Chapter 8
When Teachers and Staffs Activate Children's Wounds
Why Power Struggles Escalate Instead of Resolve

Children do not escalate in isolation.

Escalation is almost always developmental. It happens in response to how power, tone, and emotion are exchanged in a moment.

Many teachers and adults believe escalation begins with a child's behavior.
Psychology shows that escalation often begins when a child's nervous system senses threat, even if no harm was intended.

How Adults Accidentally Activate Childhood Wounds

Children who have experienced fear, control, or emotional harm are constantly scanning for danger.

They are sensitive to:

- Tone
- Facial expression
- Body language
- Volume
- Power shifts

When an adult:

- Raises their voice
- Uses sarcasm
- Embarrasses a child publicly
- Demands compliance immediately

- Challenges a child's dignity

the child's nervous system does not hear instruction.

It hears threat.

And when a child feels threatened, learning shuts down.

The Moment Things Go Wrong: Competing to Win

One of the fastest ways to escalate a child is to compete with them for power or control. This often sounds like:

- "Watch your tone when you speak to me."
- "You're not running this classroom."
- "You're crossing a line right now."
- "Try me and see what happens."
- "You're not going to challenge me."

In that moment, something subtle but powerful happens.

The professional adult steps back.

And the adult's inner child steps forward.

When an adult argues with a child to win, the interaction is no longer about guidance or safety.

It becomes personal.

Psychologically, this happens when:

- The adult feels disrespected
- Authority feels threatened
- Old feelings of powerlessness are triggered
- Shame or humiliation surfaces

At that point, the adult is no longer responding as a regulated professional.

They are reacting from a younger, wounded place.

So now:

- The child's inner child is fighting for control
- The adult's inner child is fighting for dignity

Two nervous systems collide.

And the situation escalates.

Why Some Children Escalate When Adults Argue With Them

A child cannot win against an adult.

So when they feel challenged, cornered, or shamed, their body chooses one of three survival responses:

Fight

Definition:
Fight is a survival response in which the nervous system moves toward confrontation to regain a sense of control or safety.

What's happening internally:
The brain perceives threat. The body releases stress hormones to prepare for defense. Thinking narrows. The goal is to stop the threat or reassert power.

What fight looks like in students:

- Arguing or talking back
- Yelling, cursing, or name-calling

- Defiance or refusal
- Provoking authority
- Physical aggression

Key point for educators:
The survival responses are not choice, they are reflexes. And how an adult responds to them is a choice.

Flight

Definition:
Flight is a survival response in which the nervous system attempts to escape perceived danger physically or emotionally.

What's happening internally:
The body believes safety requires distance. Stress hormones mobilize the body to get away. Attention shifts toward avoidance.

What flight looks like in students:

- Leaving the room or asking to go out repeatedly
- Avoiding work
- Frequent bathroom visits
- Skipping class
- Daydreaming or disengaging

Freeze

Definition:
Freeze is a survival response in which the nervous system shuts down to survive overwhelming threat.

What's happening internally:
The body believes neither fighting nor fleeing will keep it safe. Stress hormones spike, then drop. The system immobilizes.

What freeze look like in students:

- Blank stare
- Silence
- Inability to answer questions
- Appearing "checked out"
- Sudden drop in participation

Key point for educators:
Freeze is often misread as laziness, apathy, or defiance. It is actually overloaded.

What This Looks Like on the Outside

When a child's wound is activated, you may see:

- Defiance
- Yelling
- Refusal
- Mocking
- Shutdown
- Aggression

Both are signals, not character flaws.

Why Teachers Get Triggered

When students' survival responses are activated, they do not exist in isolation. They meet the nervous system of the adult in the room. For teachers who carry their own history of adverse childhood experiences, this moment can land with unexpected force.

This reaction is not about competence. It is about memory held in the body, the old urgency to regain safety, restore order, and prevent escalation before things spiral out of control. When a student's behavior signals threat, resistance, or unpredictability, a teacher's nervous system may respond before conscious thought has time to intervene. This is not a character flaw. It is what happens when two nervous systems shaped by stress meet in one room, and behavior becomes the language both are using to survive.

Many teachers were once children who learned very specific lessons about safety:

- Compliance kept them out of trouble
- Silence was equated with respect
- Emotional expression led to punishment rather than comfort
- Public correction carried shame
- Control was necessary to avoid consequences

Those lessons do not disappear in adulthood. They remain quietly stored, shaping how authority, disruption, and disrespect are felt in the body.

This is where trauma takes the wheel.

Chapter 9

How Nervous Systems Respond to Disrespect in the Classroom

Regulation, Authority, and the Moment of Choice

Children do not enter classrooms as blank slates. They arrive with nervous systems shaped by experience, especially experiences marked by instability, loss, or chronic stress.

For some students, authority feels unpredictable. Correction can feel like rejection. Boundaries may register as threat.

Before learning can occur, the nervous system is asking one question:

Am I safe right now?

Research in child development and trauma neuroscience shows that when a child perceives danger, the brain shifts into survival mode. The amygdala, which process emotions especially fear, threat, and survival responses, activates stress hormones rise. As a result access to the prefrontal cortex, the control center of the brain which is responsible for impulse control, reasoning, and decision-making becomes limited.

In this state, behavior intensifies, not because a child chooses disruption, but because the nervous system prioritizes protection.

Children Regulate Through Co-Regulation

Children stabilize through the adults around them. A steady adult presence communicates safety more powerfully than any instruction.

Regulation is supported by:

- calm adult demeanor
- predictable patterns
- structured connection
- clear boundaries
- protection of dignity

When these conditions are present, behavior often settles, not because the child is controlled, but because the nervous system is no longer in defense.

Teachers Are Not Outside This Biology

Responding to student behavior is not only cognitive work. It is physiological.

This chapter focuses on what happens inside a teacher when disrespect appears, and how to respond in ways that preserve authority without escalation.

By the time a student talks back, refuses a directive, or challenges authority, the moment is already charged. Urgency rises. Patience narrows. The need to act feels immediate.

This reaction is a human response to holding authority under pressure.

Why Disrespect Activates Teachers

Teaching places adults in a visible position of responsibility. When a student challenges authority, especially publicly, it disrupts order and credibility.

The nervous system reacts automatically. Disrespect signals threat to role, stability, and leadership.

Feeling a surge of anger, urgency, or defensiveness does not mean a teacher is unprofessional. It means the body is responding to perceived threat in a role that demands control and accountability.

The difference among teachers is not whether activation occurs. It is how intense it feels and how quickly it takes over.

Where ACE History Changes the Experience

For teachers with ACE histories, moments of disrespect often carry additional weight. The reaction is layered with earlier experiences where authority, safety, and control were tied to punishment, shame, or instability.

The body responds faster because it learned long ago that these moments mattered.

This is not fragility.
It is threat detection shaped by experience.

The question shifts from:
What is wrong with me? to What just got activated, and what does this moment require?

The Moment of Choice

Every moment of disrespect creates a choice even when it does not feel like one.

The choice is not whether to respond.
The choice is where the response comes from.

A threat-driven reaction focuses on shutting behavior down, regaining control, or winning the moment.

A regulated response focuses on restoring order without escalation.

This is not a strategy difference.
It is a neurological one.

Separating Meaning From Management

Disrespect requires management.
It does not require immediate emotional action.

A regulated teacher separates:

Meaning asks: *What does this behavior represent personally?*
Management asks: *What does this situation require right now?*

A student rolling their eyes may feel personal, but the management need may simply be to redirect and continue instruction.

Management may include:

- pausing instruction
- reinforcing a boundary
- redirecting behavior
- addressing the issue later

Meaning does not need to be acted out in front of students.

This separation protects authority.

Responding From Authority

Authority does not require intensity.
It requires steadiness.

It sounds like:

- "We'll address this after class."
- "You can be upset. You cannot speak to me that way."

These responses:

1. Name the boundary
2. Slow the interaction
3. Keep the teacher out of threat mode

Nothing is lost by delaying escalation.
Much is lost by reacting from it.

Regulation Is Leadership

Regulation is not the absence of reaction.
It is the ability to lead while activated.

Children regulate through co-regulation.
Adults regulate through self-regulation.

Children express distress outwardly.
Adults are responsible for managing theirs.

This is not about suppressing emotion.
It is about deciding who carries responsibility for safety.

Regulation allows teachers to:

- hold boundaries without humiliation
- correct behavior without power struggles
- maintain authority without escalating conflict

This is leadership under pressure.

Why This Matters

When teachers understand that reactions to disrespect are biological and expected, shame loosens its grip and choice becomes possible.

Disrespect will still happen.
Triggers will still arise.

But teachers who recognize activation:

- stabilize the classroom
- protect authority
- prevent escalation
- reduce emotional exhaustion

Leadership is not about preventing triggers.
It is about recognizing activation and choosing to lead anyway.

Chapter 10

Trust-Building With Students Who Resist Adults

Safety, Regulation, and the Psychology of Real Learning

Students do not trust teachers because of credentials, titles, or rules posted on the wall.
They trust based on experience.

Trust is not announced.
It is detected.

Students, especially those who have experienced instability, trauma, or repeated academic failure, are highly attuned to whether an adult is genuine, regulated, and safe. They are constantly reading tone, posture, pacing, facial expression, and consistency. Long before they respond to instruction, they respond to the adult's nervous system.

Trust Begins With Regulation

The difference between a professional adult and a wounded adult is not found in words.
It is found in presence.

A regulated adult:

- remains steady under pressure
- does not compete with children
- sets boundaries calmly
- protects dignity
- responds rather than reacts

A dysregulated adult:

- feels personally challenged
- escalates emotionally
- seeks control through authority
- argues, corrects publicly, or reacts quickly

Children sense this difference immediately.
A regulated adult signals safety.
A reactive adult signals threat.

Learning cannot occur in the presence of perceived threat. When students feel exposed, embarrassed, or emotionally unsafe, the brain shifts into defense. Cognitive resources move away from reasoning and toward survival. In contrast, when students feel safe and respected, the brain remains open to learning, problem-solving, and persistence.

Safety is not softness.
It is the foundation for cognition.

What This Looks Like in a Classroom

A student sighs loudly, leans back in their chair, and says, "This is stupid. I'm not doing this."

The room shifts. Students glance at the teacher. The moment is charged.

Two different responses can happen.

Response driven by reaction

The teacher feels challenged. Their shoulders tense. Their voice sharpens.

"Excuse me? You don't talk like that in my classroom. If you don't want to do the work, you can leave."

The student smirks and pushes the paper away. A power struggle begins. The class stops thinking about the lesson and starts watching the conflict.

Compliance may come.
But trust is lost.

The student learns: authority responds with threat.

Response driven by regulation

The teacher pauses. Breath slows. Voice remains steady.

"That assignment feels frustrating right now. You can start with the first question or take a minute and then try again."

No lecture.
No public correction.
No emotional escalation.

The student rolls their eyes but stays seated. After a moment, they pick up the pencil.

Nothing dramatic happened.

But everything changed.

The class learns:

- the teacher is steady under pressure
- mistakes do not trigger humiliation
- resistance does not create chaos
- the room is emotionally safe

This is how trust forms.
Not through speeches but through regulated moments.

Students are always learning how adults respond under pressure. When a teacher remains regulated, the nervous system of the room settles and learning remains possible.

Regulation is not personality.
It is professional practice.

Respect Is Not a Strategy; It Is a Mindset

Students quickly determine whether respect is conditional. They notice:

- who receives patience and who receives irritation
- whose mistakes are treated as learning and whose as failure
- whether dignity is preserved during correction

Respect communicates safety more powerfully than kindness alone. When dignity is protected, students are more willing to take risks, ask questions, and remain engaged.

Trust deepens when students know they are being seen with accuracy and dignity

Predictability Builds Security

Students trust environments where responses are consistent and expectations are clear. Predictability reduces anxiety and allows attention to shift from self-protection to learning.

Predictability includes:

- clear routines
- consistent boundaries
- steady emotional responses
- follow-through on promises

When students can anticipate how an adult will respond, they stop scanning for danger.

Repair Builds Credibility

Trust is not built through perfection.
It is built through accountability.

When teachers misjudge a student, respond too harshly, or make an error, repair strengthens trust more than flawless behavior ever could.

A simple repair:

- "I misunderstood you."
- "I responded too quickly."
- "Let's reset."

These moments demonstrate that authority can be responsible and safe.

Why Trust Matters More Than Control

Compliance does not equal trust.
Students may comply out of fear, avoidance, or exhaustion.

Trust produces something different:

- cooperation
- persistence
- risk-taking
- honesty

When students trust a teacher, they are willing to struggle publicly, admit confusion, and try again after failure. That is where real learning lives.

Understanding Resistance

Some students do not arrive ready to trust adults. They enter guarded, skeptical, and prepared to defend themselves. These students are often labeled defiant, oppositional, or unmotivated.

But resistance is not the problem.
Resistance is information.

Students who resist adults often carry histories of:

- inconsistent caregiving
- broken promises
- humiliation by authority
- punitive discipline without repair
- emotionally unpredictable adults

They learned early that adults were unsafe. Resistance became protection.

What looks like defiance is often self-preservation.

What Resistance Looks Like

Students who distrust adults may:

- test limits quickly
- reject praise
- challenge authority publicly
- refuse help
- appear indifferent or hostile
- shut down when corrected

These behaviors are not attempts to control the classroom. They are attempts to control exposure.

The Mistake That Breaks Trust Before It Forms

Many teachers attempt to "win over" resistant students quickly. They:

- push connection too fast
- offer praise that feels insincere
- demand respect before safety exists
- take resistance personally

For students who distrust adults, speed feels unsafe.

Trust cannot be rushed.
It is built through consistency, not persuasion.

What Builds Trust With Resistant Students

1. **Predictability over warmth**
   Consistency establishes safety; warmth becomes meaningful once stability is present.
2. **Neutral tone during correction**
   Tone communicates safety more than words.
3. **Private correction**
   Dignity reduces threat and prevents power struggles.
4. **Do not compete for control**
   Power struggles reinforce distrust.
5. **Offer structured choice**
   Choice restores agency while maintaining boundaries.

6. **Acknowledge effort instead of praising identity**
   Acknowledgment feels safer than celebration.

The Power of Presence

Students do not need perfect teachers.
They need regulated ones.

The safest adult in the room is not the loudest or most authoritative. It is the one whose nervous system remains steady when others are not.

When adults stop competing, children begin to settle.
When dignity is protected, resistance softens.
When responses are predictable, anxiety decreases.

Trust appears quietly:

- resistance decreases
- eye contact lasts longer
- effort increases
- help is accepted

These are not small shifts.
They are the beginning of change.

Students do not trust authority because it is asserted.
They trust it because it feels safe.

Trust grows when teachers:

- remain regulated
- protect dignity
- stay consistent

- repair when needed
- refuse to compete for control

When students feel safe, respected, and seen, learning becomes possible.

And when trust is present, education is no longer something done to students. It becomes something they are willing to engage in with you.

Chapter 11

Where Classroom and Family Realities Meet

Understanding the Parent Side of the Conversation

In the previous chapters, the focus has been on students and how their behavior, resistance, withdrawal, and emotional intensity often reflect needs and experiences that are not immediately visible in the classroom.

Teachers have been asked to look beyond the surface and consider what may be happening internally for the child.

But students do not exist in isolation.
They come from families.
They return each day to homes shaped by stress, responsibility, history, and survival.

To fully understand what unfolds in the classroom, teachers must also understand the adults raising the children they teach.

When a student struggles academically or behaviorally, attention naturally turns toward the home. Teachers reach out. Communication begins. Expectations for partnership rise.

And it is often in this moment, when school and home connect, that another layer of complexity emerges.

Many teachers assume that once a concern is shared, collaboration will follow. But for some families, that first call from school does not feel like partnership. It feels like exposure.

For parents carrying unresolved experiences with school, authority, or childhood adversity, communication from a teacher can trigger feelings of judgment, failure, or fear.

What feels routine and professional to the teacher may feel personal and threatening to the parent.

This distinction matters.

Teachers cannot sustain themselves in this profession if every parent response is interpreted as indifference, hostility, or lack of care. Misinterpretation leads to frustration. Frustration leads to resentment. Resentment leads to burnout.

This section shifts the lens from the student to the parent, not to excuse harmful patterns or lower expectations, but to deepen understanding so teachers can navigate family dynamics without absorbing unnecessary emotional strain.

Teachers are not only managing student learning and behavior. They are also navigating the emotional realities of the adults raising those students.

Understanding parents does not mean agreeing with everything or removing accountability. It means responding with clarity and perspective rather than reaction.

When teachers understand what may be happening on the other side of a phone call, email, or conference table, they gain something essential for longevity in this profession:

Perspective.

And perspective is one of the most powerful protections against burnout.

With this shift in focus, we begin by examining what happens in that first moment of contact between school and home and why it often carries more emotional weight than either side expects.

When the Call Home Feels Like a Threat

Teachers are trained to see communication with parents as partnership.
A phone call home.
An email.
A conference request.

These actions are meant to support the child.

But for many parents, a call from school does not feel like collaboration.
It feels like exposure.
Judgment.
Confirmation of a fear they already carry quietly.

When a student struggles academically or behaviorally, teachers often interpret silence from home as indifference:

"They don't care."
"They never respond."
"They don't show up."

But in many cases, what looks like avoidance is a survival response.

Parents who carry their own childhood adversity often experience school communication as:

- A reminder of their own academic challenges
- Proof that they are "not good enough" as a parent
- Fear of being blamed, judged, or exposed
- Anxiety about not knowing how to fix the problem

Silence is not always a neglect.
Sometimes it's just fear.

Psychology consistently shows that when shame is activated, people withdraw, deflect, or shut down not because they don't care, but because they feel incapable of responding safely.

Why School Can Trigger Old Wounds In Parents

For many adults, school was not a place of confidence.
It was a place of comparison.
Correction.
Embarrassment.
Or quiet failure.

A call from school can reactivate those memories instantly.

It can sound less like:
"Let's work together."

And more like:
"Something is wrong with your child."
"You are not doing enough."
"You are failing as a parent."

Even when those words are never spoken.

Parents who struggled in school themselves may already carry a deep belief:
I am not smart enough.
I never understood school.
Teachers never liked me.

So when the school calls, the nervous system does not hear partnership.
It hears evaluation.

The Weight Many Parents Are Already Carrying

Many parents are navigating pressures teachers may never see:

• Financial stress
• Multiple jobs or unstable work schedules
• Relationship strain
• Mental health challenges
• Unresolved trauma
• Lack of support systems

They may already feel they are barely holding life together.

When a message from school arrives about behavior, grades, or concerns, it can feel like one more confirmation that they are falling short.

And when people feel they are failing in an area that matters deeply, they do not always move toward the problem.
They sometimes avoid it.

Not because they don't care.
But because they care so much that facing the problem feels unbearable.

When Silence Is Misread

Teachers are responsible for many students at once.
When communication goes unanswered, frustration is understandable.

But it is important to recognize what silence can mean.

Silence can mean:
• "I don't know what to say."
• "I don't know how to fix this."
• "I already feel like I'm failing."
• "I'm overwhelmed."

When shame and fear are activated, the brain moves into protection, not collaboration. Research in psychology consistently shows that shame leads to withdrawal, avoidance, or defensiveness rather than engagement.

This is not a character flaw.
It is a human response to perceived judgment or inadequacy.

Understanding Before Judgment

Teachers are trained to communicate concerns clearly and directly. Parents are not trained to receive them.

Most parents are repeating what they experienced growing up.
They may never have seen calm, solution-focused communication between adults and schools.
They may not have the language to express fear or uncertainty.

So they respond the only way they know how:
- avoidance
- defensiveness
- minimization
- silence

Understanding this does not excuse lack of involvement.
It provides context.

And context changes how communication begins.

When teachers understand that a parent's silence may be rooted in shame or fear, they can approach differently. With less assumption. More clarity. More humanity.

Because many parents who appear disengaged are not uncaring.
They are afraid.

Chapter 12

The Influence Teachers Already Hold

When Parents Don't Respond the Way, We Expect

By the time a teacher reaches out to a parent, something important has already happened inside that parent.

Long before a response is sent or avoided, the parent has begun an internal reckoning.

Most parents sense something is wrong before the school confirms it.

They see:

- nightly homework battles
- tears or shut down after school
- avoidance, anger, or exhaustion
- growing tension around learning

But recognition does not bring clarity.
It often brings fear.

The parent's internal dialogue begins quietly:

- *How did I miss this?*
- *Is this my fault?*
- *Should I have done something sooner?*
- *What if I don't know how to help?*

For parents who carry unresolved wounds from their own childhood, especially those shaped by school failure, criticism, or neglect, this moment strikes deeply.

It is not just concern for the child.
It is a confrontation with their own sense of adequacy.

Shame Is the Turning Point

Psychological research consistently shows that when shame is activated, people do not move toward collaboration. They move toward protection. Shame says, *I am the problem.*

This is why parents who care deeply may appear unresponsive or resistant.

Their nervous system is no longer focused on solutions.
It is focused on self-preservation.

The Fear of Being Seen as "Not Enough"

Many parents already feel stretched beyond capacity.

They may be managing:

- long work hours
- financial strain
- unstable housing
- emotional exhaustion
- mental health challenges
- unresolved trauma

When their child struggles at school, it forces a painful acknowledgment:
I may not have what this situation requires.

Why Parents Deflect

When parents say:
"He doesn't do that at home."
"She never had this issue before."

It is easy for teachers to hear denial or dishonesty.

But deflection often serves a psychological function: it creates distance from blame.

Deflection protects a fragile sense of competence in a moment when it feels under threat.

Underneath deflection is often a thought parents cannot say aloud:
I don't know how to fix it.

Deflection is not always rejection of truth.
It is often fear with nowhere to land.

Chapter 13

When Responsibility Feels Dangerous

Discipline, Fear, and Parental Helplessness

Many parents today were raised in homes where discipline was simple, immediate, and physical.

When expectations were not met, consequences often included:

- spanking
- yelling
- threats
- punishment without explanation
- fear-based compliance

Whether these practices were accepted at the time or not, they taught a clear message:

Responsibility was enforced through punishment.

There was little ambiguity about authority.
There was little discussion about emotions.
There was little room for error.

For many children, spanking or harsh discipline became the ***only*** model of responsibility they understood.

When the Old Model Disappears

As adults, these same individuals are now parents in a very different world.

They are told that physical punishment can be harmful.
They are warned that discipline can be misinterpreted.

They are surrounded by stories of investigations, reports, and consequences.

But here is the gap that leaves many parents stuck:

The old model was removed, but no new model was truly taught.

Many parents were never shown:

- how to set firm limits without fear
- how to correct behavior without punishment
- how to stay regulated while enforcing consequences
- how to repair after conflict

So when they are told, "You need to discipline your child," they are left with an unspoken panic:

Discipline how?

The Fear Behind "I Don't Know What to Do"

For some parents, responsibility feels dangerous because they believe that one wrong move could cost them everything.

They may fear:

- being reported to child protective services
- legal consequences
- losing custody
- being labeled abusive
- their child saying something at school that is misunderstood

This fear is not abstract.
It is often rooted in lived experience, either their own or what they witnessed growing up.

For these parents, discipline no longer feels like guidance.
It feels like exposure.

So responsibility becomes paralyzing.

When Helplessness Replaces Authority

Without a safe model for discipline, many parents fall into a painful position:

They know their child needs structure.
They know behavior is escalating.
They know consistency matters.

But they also believe:
If I discipline, I could get in trouble.
If I don't discipline, things will get worse.

Caught between a rock and a hard place. This battle between fear and responsibility causes many parents to activate survival response freeze.

This can look like:

- repeated warnings without follow-through
- giving in to stop escalation
- inconsistent consequences
- avoiding conflict entirely

From the classroom, it may look like permissiveness or lack of accountability.

From the home, it often feels like helplessness.

What Teachers Need to Hold

Teachers are not responsible for teaching parents how to parent.

But teachers do need to understand this truth:

Some parents are not refusing responsibility.
They are afraid of it.

This understanding allows teachers to:

- stop personalizing lack of follow-through
- reduce frustration rooted in misinterpretation
- communicate expectations without intensifying fear
- protect their own emotional energy

Responsibility works best when people feel safe enough to carry it.

When fear is reduced, responsibility becomes possible again.

They are navigating systems that demand accountability from everyone, often without providing safety for anyone.

Understanding that collision is essential for teacher survival.

Understanding does not mean absorbing responsibility.
It means carrying only what belongs to you.

Understanding this helps teachers avoid a common trap: waiting for parents to show up in a specific way before believing change is possible. Sometimes parents will not respond as hoped.
Sometimes they cannot.

This is where an important truth must be named.

Teachers often have more immediate influence over a student's motivation than parents.

Students spend the majority of their learning hours in classrooms. They respond to the tone, structure, expectations, and emotional climate created there. The way a teacher frames struggle, effort, and belonging shapes how students experience learning every day.

When teachers wait for parent engagement to drive motivation, they unintentionally give away the influence they already hold.

Motivation is not dependent on parent response alone.
It is built through daily interactions inside the classroom.

Recognizing this does two things at once.

It reduces the tendency to interpret parent silence as lack of care. And it restores the teacher's sense of influence, even when family engagement is inconsistent.

Chapter 14

Navigating Challenging Parents While Staying Professional

When a Parent Believes the Child First

One of the most emotionally difficult moments for teachers occurs when a student tells a parent that the teacher is "picking on them," and the parent immediately enters the conversation in attack mode without seeking understanding, context, or clarification.

This situation is deeply personal for teachers, because it challenges not only classroom decisions, but character, fairness, and professionalism.

Teachers must understand a difficult truth early:

Many parents will believe their child first.
And there is often nothing a teacher can do to immediately change that.

This is not always about facts.
It is about loyalty, fear, and instinct.

Some parents genuinely believe their child's version of events. Others suspect the story is incomplete or even untrue, but still defend their child publicly to avoid shame, conflict, or exposure.

In these moments, the teacher's job is not to "win" the parent over.

The teacher's job is to rely on professionalism.

The First Principle: Stay Anchored in Professional Identity

Professionalism is not defined by how others behave.
It is defined by how consistently a teacher maintains clarity, composure, and boundaries.

When a parent accuses, challenges, or speaks from emotion, teachers may feel:

- personally attacked
- disrespected
- unsupported
- frustrated

These reactions are human.

But reacting emotionally often escalates the situation and reduces credibility.

A teacher's strength in these moments is not persuasion.
It is steadiness.

Before responding:

- slow the pace internally
- separate feelings from goals
- focus on the student, not the accusation

Professionalism begins with regulation.

Understand the Dynamic Before Responding

When a parent hears that their child feels targeted, something activates immediately:

- protective instinct

- fear their child is being treated unfairly
- concern about emotional harm
- their own past experiences with school authority

This activation happens quickly, often before facts are explored.

Teachers often assume:
"If I explain clearly, the parent will understand."

But this is not always true.

Parents are not entering as neutral investigators.
They are entering as protectors.

And protectors defend first.

Step 1: Do Not Try to Convince, Stay Clear

The fastest way to escalate the situation is to argue against the parent's belief.

Trying to "prove" the child is wrong often:

- increases defensiveness
- turns the conversation into a power struggle
- positions teacher vs parent

Instead, stay grounded in observable reality.

Use language like:

"I want to share what I'm seeing in class so we can support your child."

This avoids accusation. It centers the student and keeps the conversation professional. Clarity is more effective than persuasion.

Step 2: Acknowledge Without Agreeing

Parents often need to feel heard before they can listen.

Acknowledgment does not mean agreement.

It sounds like:

- "I hear your concern."
- "I understand why this would be upsetting."
- "I can see this matters to you."

This lowers emotional intensity without conceding accuracy.

Step 3: Return the Focus to the Student

When conversations become personal, redirect.

"Our shared goal is helping your child succeed."
"I want to make sure your child feels supported and successful in class."
"Let's look at what will help your child move forward."

The student, not the accusation, remain the center.

Step 4: Accept That You May Not Be Believed

This is one of the hardest realities for teachers.

Even with documentation…
Even with professionalism…
Even with clarity…

Some parents will still side with their child.

This does not mean the teacher has failed.
It means the parent-child bond is operating as expected.

Teachers cannot control belief.
They can control professionalism.

Step 5: Avoid the Trap of Proving Yourself

Trying to defend every decision often drains emotional energy and rarely changes perception.

Instead:

- state observations
- explain expectations
- outline next steps

Then stop trying to persuade.

Professional credibility builds through consistency, not argument.

Step 6: Set Boundaries When Needed

If communication becomes disrespectful:

- remain calm
- restate purpose
- redirect or pause

Examples:

"I want this conversation to stay productive and focused on your child."
"I'm committed to working together, but I need us to keep this respectful."
"If now isn't a good time, we can continue later."

Boundaries protect professionalism.

Step 7: Document and Use Support Systems

Teachers should not manage high-conflict situations alone.

Professional practice includes:

- documenting communication
- involving administration when necessary
- following school protocols

Documentation:

- protects the teacher
- protects the student
- maintains transparency

A Grounded Truth Teachers Need to Hear

Sometimes, parents know their child is not being fully truthful.

But they still defend them.

Not because they believe every detail,
but because protecting their child feels safer than confronting them.

Understanding this helps teachers avoid personalizing the interaction.

This is not about you.
It is about a parent navigating loyalty, fear, and identity.

Teachers cannot control how parents respond.

But they can control:

- their own tone
- their clarity
- their boundaries
- their professionalism

And professionalism, maintained under pressure, protects more than authority.

It protects longevity in the profession.

Because the goal is not to win every interaction.

The goal is to remain steady enough to keep doing the work that matters most, supporting students.

Chapter 15

When Adult Workplace Dynamics Mirror Adolescence

When Integrity Meets Insecurity in School Communities

Most new teachers enter the profession believing the hardest challenges will involve students, curriculum, and classroom management. Few expect the most confusing moments to come from adult interactions in the staff room, hallways, meetings, or text threads.

Yet many school environments quietly reproduce familiar social roles:

- the colleague who dominates conversations or dismisses others
- the observer who stays silent to avoid conflict
- the teacher who becomes the target of subtle criticism
- and the one who speaks up for fairness, often at personal cost

For teachers who occupy that last role, the experience can feel isolating. When leadership avoids conflict or fails to address professional conduct directly. Advocating for integrity can become emotionally draining.

This is not about student behavior.
It is about adult dynamics that unfold in spaces where professionalism, collaboration, and emotional responsibility are expected.

Adult bullying in schools rarely looks obvious. It does not usually involve shouting, threats, or visible confrontation. Instead, it appears through everyday interactions.

A new teacher might notice:

- being left out of planning conversations that affect their grade level
- colleagues sharing inside information but not including them
- hearing, "We don't do it that way here," without explanation
- being corrected publicly rather than privately
- noticing laughter after they leave a room without understanding why

The colleague creating this environment may appear:

- confident in meetings
- well-connected to administration
- vocal about school expectations
- helpful on the surface

Their influence often comes from social positioning, not formal authority.

The teacher who becomes a target is often the last to recognize what is happening.
These educators tend to be:

- dependable and organized
- willing to help anyone who asks

- focused on students rather than politics
- respectful of procedures
- eager to learn and improve

They often think:

- *I'm doing my job.*
- *I meet deadlines.*
- *I follow expectations.*
- *There's no reason for anyone to have an issue with me.*

Because their approach is transparent, they do not anticipate manipulation.

In practice, targeting can look like:

- a colleague telling administration, "I'm concerned about their classroom management," without ever speaking to the teacher directly
- being given incorrect information about procedures, then question the teacher in front of administrator to reveal that the teacher is not following protocol
- being encouraged to vent about leadership, then having those comments repeated out of context
- colleagues forming planning groups and excluding one teacher without explanation
- being the last to receive updates that everyone else already knows

Over time, the teacher may feel:

- confused about shifting expectations

- anxious before meetings
- unsure who to trust
- hesitant to ask questions
- emotionally exhausted despite doing their job well

The most painful part is often not the behavior itself, but the lack of clarity. Something feels wrong, but it cannot be easily named.

Teacher preparation programs train educators in instruction, assessment, and classroom management. They rarely prepare them for adult workplace culture.

Research consistently shows teachers leave schools more often because of workplace climate than because of students.

Key factors include:

- lack of collegial support
- ongoing tension with colleagues
- exclusion from decision-making
- unsupportive or avoidant leadership
- environments where conflict is ignored rather than addressed

A professional title does not remove insecurity. Adults bring their personal histories, identity needs, and unresolved experiences into their work.

In school settings, insecurity can show up through:

- social comparison ("Whose class is doing better?")
- competition for recognition

- forming alliances for protection or influence
- subtle undermining of colleagues perceived as confident or independent

For example:

- A teacher admired by students may trigger jealousy.
- A new teacher with strong organization may unintentionally highlight others' disorganization.
- A quiet, self-contained teacher may be perceived as distant or judgmental.

These reactions are rarely about misconduct.
They are responses to perceived threat.

Leadership also plays a critical role. In environments where expectations for adult conduct are unclear:

- cliques form
- gossip becomes normalized
- concerns are handled indirectly
- professional boundaries blur

Without accountability, harmful patterns grow quietly.

How to Navigate It

Understanding these dynamics is a form of protection.
It allows teachers to respond thoughtfully rather than internalize a problem that does not belong to them.

A new teacher can remain grounded by focusing on concrete practices:

1. Stay anchored in your role.
Prioritize instruction, preparation, and student support. Let your work remain your foundation.

2. Seek clarity early.
If expectations feel inconsistent, ask direct, neutral questions:
"Can you clarify the process for this?"
"Is there a written guideline I should follow?"

3. Avoid informal venting.
Complaints shared casually can be repeated later. Keep conversations professionally and solution-focused.

4. Document important communication.
Follow verbal conversations with brief confirmation emails:
"Thank you for clarifying. I'll proceed as discussed."

5. Build intentional connections.
Identify colleagues who demonstrate consistency, professionalism, and support. Collaboration should feel steady, not political.

6. Use leadership channels when needed.
If patterns affect your ability to work effectively, bring specific examples, not emotion, to appropriate administrator.

7. Maintain boundaries.
You do not need to participate in gossip, alliances, or social positioning to belong.

Support is not a sign of weakness.
It is a professional strategy.

Teachers who lead with integrity often struggle most in environments shaped by insecurity not because they lack strength, but because they expect honesty and fairness.

Recognizing these dynamics does not eliminate difficulty.
But it reduces confusion and prevents unnecessary self-doubt.

You may not be able to control staff culture.
But you can control how you stand within it.

Remain steady.
Protect your professionalism.
Stay aligned with your purpose.

Because the presence of insecurity in others should never diminish the value of the work you came to do.

Chapter 16

For the Teacher Who Feels Threatened by a Colleague's Success

Understanding What You Can't See, Yet

If another teacher's confidence, efficiency, or popularity with students makes you feel uneasy, irritated, or defensive, pause.

This section is not here to judge you.
It is here to help you understand what your nervous system may be doing without your permission.

Feeling threatened does not make you a bad educator.
Ignoring it can quietly sabotage your growth, your relationships, and your career.

What Research Tells Us About Insecurity at Work

Psychological research consistently shows that threat perception is often internal, not external.

When people feel uncertain about their competence, belonging, or worth, the brain shifts into a protective mode. Instead of learning, it scans for comparison, danger, and status loss.

This is not a character flaw.
It is a **survival response**.

In educational settings, where evaluation, visibility, and comparison are constant, this response is especially common.

What the Insecure Nervous System Is Protecting

If another teacher's success bothers you, your nervous system may be protecting you from:

- **Shame** ("What if I'm not good enough?")
- **Fear of exposure** ("What if others see my struggles?")
- **Fear of comparison** ("What if I fall behind?")
- **Fear of replacement** ("What if I become less valued?")
- **Fear of being unseen** ("Why aren't students responding to me like that?")

The brain experiences these fears as threat—even if no one is attacking you.

So it looks for relief.

How Insecurity Quietly Turns Into Self-Sabotage

When insecurity goes unexamined, it often shows up as behaviors that feel justified in the moment—but damage you over time.

Research on workplace dynamics and defense mechanisms shows common patterns such as:

- Minimizing a colleague's success
- Finding fault where none is required
- Withholding collaboration
- Aligning with others to validate discomfort
- Interpreting neutral behavior as arrogance
- Avoiding growth opportunities out of comparison
- Resenting rather than learning

These behaviors do not protect your status.

They isolate you.

The Blind Spot: What You May Not Realize

Here is the hard truth insecurity hides:

The colleague you feel threatened by is not taking anything from you.

They are revealing something **you may need to tend to in yourself**.

Your nervous system may be confusing:

- Their confidence with judgment of you
- Their ease with criticism of you
- Their success with your failure

This is a false equation, but the body believes it.

Awareness is the interrupt.

What Research Says Actually Restores Confidence

1. Self-Efficacy Is Built Internally, Not by Comparison

Psychological research shows that confidence grows when people focus on mastery and growth, not relative ranking.

Ask:

- What skill do I want to strengthen next?
- What support would help me grow?
- What am I already doing well?

Comparison drains energy.
Mastery builds it.

2. Curiosity Deactivates Threat Responses

Neuroscience shows that curiosity shifts the brain out of defense and back into learning.

Instead of: "Why are they like that?"

Ask: "What are they doing that works?"

This is not submission.
It is self-investment.

3. Emotional Regulation Improves Professional Perception

Research on emotional intelligence shows that people who regulate their reactions are perceived as more competent, trustworthy, and collaborative—regardless of raw performance.

Your regulation is visible.
So is dysregulation.

4. Projection Shrinks When Feelings Are Named

Studies on projection show that naming emotions reduces the urge to act them out.

Try:

- *"I feel threatened."*
- *"I feel insecure."*
- *"I feel behind."*

Naming is not weakness.
It is containment.

Questions That Disrupt Self-Sabotage

Use these privately, honestly:

- What does this person's success make me fear about myself?
- Am I reacting to them or to a story I'm telling myself?
- What belief about my worth is being activated?
- What support do I need that I'm not asking for?
- How might my behavior be hurting my reputation?

These questions create **choice**.

Another teacher's success is not an indictment of you.

It is information.

It may be pointing toward:

- Burnout you haven't named
- Support you haven't received
- Skills you want to build
- Validation you're seeking externally

None of these are moral failures.

They are **signals**.

What Growth Looks Like Instead

Secure teachers:

- Learn from peers instead of competing with them
- Ask for help without shame
- Celebrate others without diminishing themselves

- Focus on their own lane
- Build competence quietly and steadily

This is not about becoming someone else.

It is about becoming less reactive and more intentional.

A Closing Truth

Insecurity does not mean you are weak.
It means you are human in a demanding system.

But when insecurity drives behavior, it quietly undermines the very things you want most:

- Respect
- Stability
- Confidence
- Belonging

Awareness is the turning point.

When you see what your nervous system has been trying to protect you from, you stop fighting others, and start strengthening yourself.

That is how teachers grow.

A Word of Encouragement

To the Administrators and Teachers Who Are Making a Difference

If you are an administrator who leads with integrity, steadiness, and care, even when it costs you, this is for you.

If you are a teacher who shows up early, stays late, pours into students, and rarely hears "thank you," this is for you.

If your work feels invisible, misunderstood, or quietly heavy, hear this:

You are not insignificant.

You are not replaceable.

And you are not forgotten, no matter how it feels.

There is a larger story unfolding than test scores, emails, evaluations, or public narratives. Education has always about humanity before it was about systems.

What you do matters because people matter.

The Bigger Play

Not every contribution shows up immediately.
Not every impact is measured.
Not every seed grows where you can see it.

Education works on a timeline that is longer than recognition.

Sometimes the effect of your patience appears years later, in a student who remembers feeling safe, capable, or seen when their world felt unstable. Sometimes it shows up in a quiet confidence that took root because someone believed when it mattered most.

You are shaping nervous systems.
You are modeling regulation.
You are teaching children what safe adults look like.

That kind of work does not trend on social media.
But it changes lives.

Not Everyone Can Do This Work

This is important to say plainly:

Not everyone can do this job.

It requires:

- Emotional endurance
- Cognitive flexibility
- Moral courage
- Patience without guarantee
- Care without constant return

This is not accidental.

If you are here, still caring, still trying, still reflecting, there is something particular about you. A capacity. A calling. A strength that was not given randomly.

Education does not call the loudest voices.
It calls the steadfast ones.

For Teachers Working Without Praise or Recognition

There are seasons in education where affirmation is scarce and demands are endless. In those seasons, it is easy to confuse silence with insignificance.

Please don't.

Your value is not determined by applause.
Your worth is not measured by visibility.

Sometimes the most important work happens quietly:

- When you keep your tone calm

- When you choose patience over reaction
- When you notice a child who is disappearing
- When you remain steady even when no one is watching

Those moments shape outcomes more than any metric ever could.

For Administrators Leading With Care

If you are an administrator who:

- Protects teachers
- Regulates yourself under pressure
- Reflects instead of retaliates
- Uplifts instead of controls
- Chooses humanity alongside standards

You are doing sacred work.

You may not always be celebrated for it. Sometimes ethical leadership makes me feel lonely. But your steadiness creates safety, and safety is where good teaching survives.

Your impact multiplies far beyond your office.

A Letter to Future Educators

To the future educators who have hesitated, paused, or reconsidered this path because of headlines, social media, or public discourse, your questions are understandable.

Education is often portrayed as broken, exhausting, thankless, and impossible. And yes, this profession carries weight. It always has.

But there is a truth that deserves to be spoken honestly.

Teaching is one of the few professions where a single adult can change the trajectory of a child's life. Not through grand gestures, but through consistency, patience, and the quiet daily work of believing in students who may not yet believe in themselves.

You will not fix every problem in education. No single teacher can. But you will create moments that matter, moments where a child feels seen, understood, and capable.

Those moments last longer than headlines.

But here is a truth that deserves honesty:

Trauma exists in every industry.
It does not disappear when you change careers.
It follows unexamined wounds wherever people go.

What matters is not finding a place without challenge but finding a place where meaning lives.

And meaning lives in education.

It lives in:

- Watching a child grow from month to month
- Seeing confidence form where fear once lived
- Witnessing curiosity ignite

- Being present for transformation that is real, human, and alive

There is joy here that cannot be replicated elsewhere.

Quiet joy. Deep joy. Purposeful joy.

The Difference Is Awareness

Education does not require perfection.
It requires awareness.

When educators understand trauma, both their students' and their own, they gain choice. They learn to notice what is working, what is meaningful, and what deserves protection.

The goal is not to endure suffering.
The goal is to work with clarity, humanity, and hope.

If you are here, reading this, reflecting, questioning, caring,

You are part of something larger than any policy cycle or public narrative. You are part of the long, quiet story of people who chose to show up for others when it mattered.

That story continues because of you.

And that is enough.

Chapter 17
When Trauma Comes From Above
How Administrators Can Activate Wounds in Teachers

Many administrators are intelligent, driven, and highly accomplished. They understand curriculum, data, and policy. They know how to run systems and meet mandates.

But achievement does not automatically mean emotional health.

Like teachers, many administrators are leading while carrying unresolved trauma. And when that trauma meets a teacher's trauma, the classroom becomes unbearable, not because of students, but because of power.

This chapter is about naming a reality that many teachers live quietly.

When Leadership Is Filtered Through Trauma

Trauma does not disappear when someone earns a title.
It often becomes harder to see, especially when it is rewarded.

In leadership, unresolved trauma frequently hides behind:

- Perfectionism
- Control
- Rigid expectations
- Emotional distance
- Inflexibility
- Harsh communication

An administrator operating from unresolved trauma may sincerely believe they are firm, professional, or high-expectation, while unknowingly creating fear, instability, or emotional harm.

When leadership is driven by fear rather than regulation, the entire system feels unsafe.

What looks like decisiveness may actually be self-protection.
What looks like confidence may be armor.
What looks like authority may be a nervous system attempting to stabilize itself through control.

Why This Hits Teachers So Hard

Teachers are not in positions of authority.

They do not control evaluations.
They do not control contracts.
They do not control assignments.
They do not control job security.

A teacher who is already managing student trauma and carrying their own has very little power to protect themselves when leadership becomes unpredictable, dismissive, or threatening.

When a teacher with trauma is overseen by an administrator with trauma, the nervous system never rests.

Teaching stops being challenging.
It becomes unbearable.

The body remains in survival mode not because of students, but because safety feels conditional.

How Administrative Trauma Shows Up

Unresolved trauma in leadership often presents in patterns rather than isolated incidents:

- Public criticism instead of private feedback
- Emotional coldness or sudden mood shifts
- Excessive micromanagement
- Unrealistic expectations with no support
- Dismissal of teacher concerns
- Inconsistent discipline policies
- Punitive responses to mistakes
- Lack of empathy disguised as "standards"

To a traumatized teacher, these behaviors do not feel professional.

They feel familiar.

They echo earlier experiences of power, control, unpredictability, or emotional harm experiences where the teacher had little agency and no protection.

Why Harmful Leadership Can Look Like Enjoyment

To teachers on the receiving end, some administrators appear to enjoy causing harm.

They document relentlessly.
They set impossible expectations.
They terminate teachers not for incompetence, but for refusal to perform emotional submission.

It feels personal.
It feels calculated.
It feels cruel.

But in many cases, what looks like enjoyment is actually relief.

Relief from internal discomfort.
Relief from feeling powerless.
Relief from unresolved shame, fear, or inadequacy.

Trauma does not always express itself as pain.
In positions of authority, it often expresses itself as control.

For an administrator with unresolved trauma, power can become a way to regulate the nervous system:

- Power soothes anxiety
- Compliance restores safety
- Dominance quiets internal chaos
- Punishment discharges emotional tension

This is maladaptive regulation.

And in many systems, it is quietly rewarded.

Ego, Threat, and the Need to Be Right

Many administrators were once high-achieving teachers themselves. Their identity is often built on:

- Competence
- Expertise
- Respect
- Being seen as the authority

When a teacher questions a decision, teaches differently, succeeds without admiration, or fails to provide ego reinforcement, the administrator's nervous system may interpret the interaction not as professional difference, but as threat.

Threat to identity.
Threat to authority.
Threat to worth.

In trauma psychology, perceived threat activates defense, not reflection.

So the response shifts:

- Increased scrutiny
- Documentation without support
- Moving goalposts
- Setting teachers up to fail
- Removing the "problem" rather than addressing insecurity

The goal is not to harm.
The goal is to silence internal discomfort.
The impact, however, is harm.

The Hyper-Controlling Administrator

Often grew up in chaos or unpredictability. Control became safety.

- Needs everything done exactly their way
- Struggles to trust teachers
- Reacts strongly to small deviations
- Sees questions as challenges

Teachers feel watched, tense, and constantly afraid of doing something wrong.

The Emotionally Detached Administrator

Often learned early that emotions were unsafe or irrelevant.

- Appears cold or dismissive
- Minimizes emotional concerns
- Avoids difficult conversations
- Priority Compliance over connection

Teachers feel invisible, unsupported, and alone.

The Reactive Administrator

Often carries unresolved anger or humiliation.

- Escalates quickly
- Uses authority to regain control
- Publicly corrects or embarrasses staff
- Shifts blame instead of reflecting

Teachers learn to stay silent, not because they agree, but because it feels unsafe to speak.

Chapter 18

How an Administrator Can Feel Threatened by a Teacher

(Without the Teacher Intending Harm)

Feeling threatened is not the same as being threatened.

In leadership psychology, threat is often internal, not external. It arises when a person's sense of competence, authority, or identity feels destabilized.

For administrators with unresolved trauma or insecure professional identity, certain teacher behaviors, while appropriate and professional can activate that threat response.

What the Teacher Is Often Doing (Unintentionally)

1. Demonstrating High Competence Without Seeking Approval

A teacher who:

- Consistently produces strong results
- Is confident in their instructional decisions
- Does not seek frequent validation
- Functions independently

May trigger insecurity in an administrator whose identity relies on being the "expert."

The threat is not the teacher's success.
It is the administrator's fear of being less necessary.

2. Asking Clarifying or Reflective Questions

Questions such as:

- "Can you explain the rationale for this change?"
- "How does this align with our stated goals?"
- "What data are we using to make this decision?"

Are professional and appropriate.

But to a trauma-affected leader, questions may feel like:

- Public challenge
- Loss of control
- Exposure of uncertainty

The nervous system interprets curiosity as confrontation.

3. Teaching Differently, but Effectively

Teachers who:

- Use innovative methods
- Adapt curriculum creatively
- Serve students in nontraditional ways
- Achieve success outside the administrator's preferred style

May unintentionally signal:

"Your way isn't the only way."

To a secure leader, this is growth.
To an insecure one, it feels like invalidating authority.

4. Not Participating in Ego Reinforcement

Some administrators unconsciously rely on:

- Praise
- Deference
- Emotional reassurance
- Visible compliance

A teacher who is respectful but not flattering may be misread as:

- Cold
- Resistant
- Disengaged
- Disrespectfully

The threat is not disrespect.
It is unmet emotional expectation.

5. Maintaining Strong Professional Boundaries

- Teachers sometimes protect themselves professionally by:
- Documenting interactions
- Referencing union or contractual language
- Requesting meetings with clear agendas
- Asking that concerns be communicated in writing

These practices are standard professional safeguards. However, to a dysregulated administrator, such boundaries may be misinterpreted as:

Distrust

- A challenge to authority
- A loss of informal control

In environments where leadership relies on ambiguity or informal power structures, clear professional boundaries can unintentionally trigger discomfort or defensiveness.

What the Administrator Is Actually Reacting To

The administrator rarely reacting to the teacher's behavior itself.

They are reacting to:

- Fear of being exposed as uncertain
- Fear of losing relevance
- Fear of losing control
- Fear of not being respected
- Fear of past failure or humiliation

That is survival masquerading as authority.

The teacher becomes a stand-in for someone from the administrator's past who:

- Challenged them
- Diminished them
- Made them feel powerless

The Critical Clarification

A teacher does not cause an administrator's trauma response.

The teacher may activate it, but activation is not responsibility.

Professional behavior does not become a threat simply because someone experiences it that way.

A Grounding Truth For Teachers:

If you are conducting yourself professionally, ethically, and competently:

- You are not responsible for managing your administrator's insecurity.
- You are not the problem.

Why This Drives Teachers Away

When competence is punished and curiosity is treated as defiance, teachers learn that:

- Safety requires silence
- Excellence invites scrutiny
- Staying small feels safer than growing

And eventually, they leave.

Chapter 19

How Unresolved Trauma Shapes Conflict Between Teachers and Leadership

When Trauma Meets Trauma

When a traumatized teacher works under a traumatized administrator, both nervous systems are activated.

The administrator feels threatened by questions or emotion. The teacher feels threatened by authority and unpredictability.

Neither feels safe.

Teaching becomes survival.

This dynamic more than workload, more than curriculum, more than students is a major, often unspoken contributor to teacher burnout and teacher shortages.

Not because teachers can't teach.

But because they cannot breathe.

Why This Feels So Personal

For many teachers, administrators unconsciously become symbolic.

They represent:

- Past authority figures
- Adults who didn't protect
- People who had power and misused it
- Voices that once silenced them

So when an administrator criticizes, dismisses, or intimidates, the teacher's reaction is often bigger than the moment.

It's not weakness.

It's memory.

An Important Truth Teachers Need to Hear

A school district is not one administrator.

A profession is not one school.

Your experience is sometimes shaped by luck, timing, and leadership fit.

This does not mean you failed.

It means you encountered a system or a leader, who could not hold you safely.

What Teachers Can Do When They Cannot Control the System

You may not be able to change leadership.

But you can become aware.

Awareness allows you to:

- Stop internalizing mistreatment
- Separate feedback from threat
- Recognize trauma-driven behavior in others
- Decide when to stay and when to leave
- Protect your nervous system
- Seek healthier environments

The goal is not endurance.

The goal is sustainability.

Learning to See Trauma Without Absorbing It

When teachers understand trauma both their own and others', they stop blaming themselves for environments that are unsafe.

They stop asking:
"What's wrong with me?"

And start asking:
"What is happening here?"

That shift restores dignity.

A teacher without authority will never fully control their experience.

But a teacher with awareness will no longer be controlled by it.

You are not weak for struggling under trauma-driven leadership.

You are human.

And the more you understand what is happening, the more power you quietly reclaim.

Chapter 20

When One Leader Changes Everything

How a Single Traumatic Experience Can Alter a Teacher's Sense of Safety

It only takes one.

One principal.
One supervisor.
One meeting behind a closed door.
One experience where power was used unpredictably, dismissively, or punitively.

Many teachers enter the profession hopefully, collaborative, and trusting. They assume leadership exists to support growth. They believe feedback is meant to help. They trust that professionalism will be met with fairness.

And then something happens.

A principal humiliates them publicly.
A supervisor twists their words.
An observation becomes punitive instead of developmental.
A concern is met with retaliation.
An evaluation feels personal rather than professional.

And from that moment on, teaching is no longer just teaching.

How One Experience Becomes a Lasting Wound

Trauma does not require repetition to take root.
When the experience involves authority, livelihood, and identity, one incident is enough.

That single experience teaches the nervous system something new:

This is not safe.

Even when the teacher moves to a new school.
Even when leadership changes.
Even when nothing is technically "wrong."

The body remembers.

When Awareness Turns Into Paranoia

After a traumatic experience with leadership, many teachers describe themselves as becoming paranoid.

But paranoia is not the most accurate word.
What they are experiencing is trauma-informed hypervigilance.

It shows up as:

- Overanalyzing emails for hidden meaning
- Assuming praise is followed by punishment
- Expecting observations to be "set-ups"
- Fear that casual conversations are being documented
- Distrust of sudden friendliness from administration
- Constantly wondering, "What did I do wrong?"

The teacher is no longer responding to the present moment.
They are responding to memory.

This is not irrational thinking.
It is a nervous system trying to prevent harm from happening again.

Why Trust Becomes So Hard to Rebuild

When harm comes from a principal or supervisor, it strikes deeper than peer conflict.

Leadership controls:

- Evaluations
- Job security
- Assignments
- Reputation
- Career trajectory

So when that power is misused even once the teacher's sense of professional safety collapses.

From that point on:

- Neutral actions feel threatening
- Silence feels ominous
- Feedback feels dangerous
- Visibility feels risky

The teacher learns to stay alert, guarded, and prepared.

Not because they want to be difficult.
But because they don't want to be blindsided again.

The Cost of Teaching in a State of Suspicion

Living in this state is exhausting.

Teaching while hypervigilant means:

- Constant tension in the body
- Difficulty being present with students
- Emotional withdrawal from colleagues
- Loss of creativity and risk-taking
- Chronic stress and burnout

Over time, teachers may begin to question themselves:

Why am I like this now?
Why can't I just let it go?

The answer is simple and painful:
Because something important was broken.

Why Others Don't Always Understand

From the outside, it may look like the teacher is:

- Overreacting
- Negative
- Resistant to leadership
- "Stuck in the past"

But what others don't see is the internal calculation happening constantly:

Is this safe?
Will this be used against me later?
What am I missing?

This constant scanning is not a personality change.
It is a survival strategy.

Chapter 21

When the Body Knows Before the Mind

How Trauma Lives in Teachers Long After the Bell Rings

Trauma does not stay neatly contained within the moments that created it.
It does not end when the meeting is over, the observation concludes, or the administrator leaves the room.

It settles into the body.

Many teachers cannot explain why their heart races before certain emails, why their stomach tightens during walkthroughs, or why exhaustion hits before the day has even begun. They tell themselves they are overreacting. They try to be rational. They remind themselves they are competent, experienced, and capable.

But trauma is not stored in logic.
It is stored in the nervous system.

Why Leaving Doesn't Always Bring Relief

Many teachers believe that once they leave a harmful school or administrator, the pain will disappear.

Sometimes it does.
Often, it doesn't.

Because trauma is not tied to a building.
It is tied to experience.

A new school may be healthier. A new administrator may be supportive. And still, the teacher flinches when called into an office. Still second-guesses praise. Still braces for impact when none is coming.

This does not mean the teacher is broken.
It means the body remembers what the mind is trying to forget.

The Grief No One Talks About

There is a quiet grief that follows trauma-driven leadership.

Grief for:

- The teacher you were before fear entered the room
- The joy that once came easily
- The confidence that didn't require constant reassurance
- The profession you loved before it became survival

Many teachers feel ashamed of this grief. They tell themselves others have it worse. They minimize their pain because no single moment seems "bad enough" to justify how deeply it affected them.

But cumulative harm is still harm.

And grief does not require permission to exist.

Relearning Safety in the Profession

Healing does not require teachers to leave education, though for some, leaving is necessary.
It requires relearning safety.

Safety looks like:

- Leadership that welcomes questions without punishment
- Feedback that is specific, private, and humane
- Boundaries that are respected
- Systems that value people, not just outcomes

And just as importantly, safety looks like internal permission:

- Permission to slow down
- Permission to trust again, carefully
- Permission to say, "That environment hurt me" without self-blame

The Difference Between Resilience and Self-Abandonment

Teachers are often praised for resilience.

But resilience becomes dangerous when it requires self-abandonment.

When teachers push through environments that harm them, ignore warning signs, or silence their intuition to appear "professional," resilience turns into endurance at the cost of the self.

Healing begins when teachers stop asking,
"How much can I tolerate?"

And start asking,
"What allows me to stay whole?"

A Quiet Reclamation

Reclaiming yourself after trauma does not happen all at once.
It happens in small, quiet ways.

It happens when:

- You notice your body and listen
- You trust discomfort as information
- You stop explaining away harm
- You choose alignment over approval

You were never meant to absorb trauma as part of your job description.
You were never meant to normalize fear as professionalism.

Your sensitivity did not make teaching harder.
It made you human in a system that forgot how to be.

And as you learn to honor what your body has been trying to tell you all along, something shifts.

Teaching stops being survival.
And slowly, it becomes yours again.

Chapter 22

How Unhealed Wounds Distort Professional Judgment

Unhealed wounds do not stay contained

Unhealed wounds rarely remain contained within a person's personal history or emotional life. When left unattended, those wounds begin to shape perception, influence judgment, and quietly determine how power is used.

A wounded person does not see the world as it is.
They see the world through the emotional lens formed at the moment the wound occurred.

And when that wounded individual holds authority whether in a school, workplace, or institution, the effects of that lens do not remain personal.

They spread.

When Pain Becomes the Lens

Professional judgment depends on clarity, the ability to assess situations based on evidence, context, and proportional response.

Trauma interferes with that process.

When wounds remain unhealed, neutral behavior feels threatening.

Control begins to feel like safety

The nervous system reacts before reason can intervene.

In these moments, decisions are no longer guided by discernment.
They are guided by protection.

This is how trauma distorts judgment, not through conscious intent, but through altered perception.

A person believes they are responding to the present moment, when in reality they are reacting to a wound formed long ago.

Trauma Does Not End With the Individual

The harm created by unhealed wounds rarely stops with the person carrying them.

In many ways, trauma behaves like a virus.

Not because it is identical in form, but because it spreads through exposure, interaction, and repetition.

When a wounded individual occupies a position of authority, such as a school administrator, supervisor, or leader, their unresolved pain can influence how they interpret behavior and how they exercise power.

They may:

- Act harshly to regain control
- Dismiss others to protect their ego
- Punish instead of reflect
- Project pain outward
- Normalize harm as "necessary leadership"

The person on the receiving end absorbs the impact.

That person now carries a wound of their own.

Unless that wound is recognized and addressed, the cycle continues.

How Trauma Replicates Itself

The process often follows a predictable pattern:

1. A wounded person harms another emotionally, psychologically, or relationally.
2. The harmed person internalizes the experience, developing fear, anger, shame, or hypervigilance.
3. That internalized wound alters their behavior, especially during moments of stress.
4. They unintentionally pass the harm forward.
5. Over time, the environment adapts to survival.

What began as one person's unresolved pain gradually reshapes the culture around them.

Why This Matters for Society

When these dynamics multiply across organizations, schools, and communities, the effects extend far beyond any single workplace.

A society shaped by unhealed wounds becomes reactive rather than thoughtful.

Judgment is replaced by assumption.
Dialogue is replaced by defensiveness.
Difference is treated as threat.

The result is a population that is:

- Easily triggered
- Quick to blame
- Resistant to accountability
- Addicted to outrage

- Detached from empathy

This is not because people are inherently worse than before.

It is because pain has been allowed to multiply unchecked.

The Turning Point: Awareness Interrupts the Spread

Unlike a virus, trauma does not require medication to stop spreading.

It requires awareness.

The cycle begins to break when individuals pause long enough to ask themselves difficult questions:

- What am I reacting to?
- Does this situation feel familiar in an old way?
- Am I responding to the present or reliving the past?
- What wound might be influencing my judgment right now?

These questions restore choice.

They return power to the present moment.

The Responsibility of Professionals

Professionals, especially those in education, leadership, and caregiving, hold influence that extends far beyond their job descriptions.

Their unhealed wounds do not remain personal.

They shape policies.
They influence workplace cultures.
They determine whether others feel safe or threatened.

This does not mean professionals must be perfect.

It means they must be self-aware.

Healing is not about erasing pain.

It is about preventing pain from being passed forward.

The lesson of this chapter is simple but profound:

Healing is not merely a private act; it is a social responsibility.

Every person who chooses reflection over reaction interrupts the cycle.

Every leader who regulates instead of retaliates reduces harm.

Every professional who tends to their own wounds protects not only themselves, but everyone they influence.

The world does not need more wounded people in positions of power.

It needs individuals willing to pause, look inward, and confront the parts of themselves that influence how they treat others.

Healing is not weakness.

It is containment.

And containment is how cycles end.

Chapter 23

What Teachers Need From Leadership

Why Regulated Administrators Create Motivated Schools

Most administrators enter leadership because they believe in education.
They value growth.
They care about outcomes.
They want teachers to succeed.

But many leaders are taught how to manage systems, not how to regulate nervous systems.

And teaching is a nervous-system profession.

Teachers perform best not when they are pressured, threatened, or monitored, but when their nervous systems feel safe, valued, and supported.

The Teacher's Nervous System at Work

Teaching requires:

- Continuous decision-making
- Emotional presence
- Cognitive flexibility
- Regulation under pressure
- Public performance
- Constant evaluation

From a neurological standpoint, teachers work under sustained cognitive and emotional load.

Research in motivation and neuropsychology shows that people perform optimally when the prefrontal cortex, the part of the brain responsible for planning, creativity, and problem-solving is online.

That only happens when the nervous system feels safe.

When teachers feel threatened, unsupported, or devalued, the brain shifts into survival mode. Performance narrows. Innovation declines. Risk-taking stops.

But when teachers feel seen and valued, the opposite occurs.

Why Assurance and Uplift Matter

Teachers do not need constant praise.
They need accurate, grounded affirmation.

Psychological research consistently shows that self-efficacy, a person's belief in their ability to succeed, directly impacts effort, persistence, and performance.

When teachers believe:

- I am capable
- My contribution matters
- My leader sees my effort

They are more likely to:

- Go beyond minimum expectations
- Innovate
- Take instructional risks
- Collaborate
- Persist through challenges

This is why uplifting leadership is not indulgent.
It is strategic.

What Happens When Teachers Feel Good About Their Work

When teachers feel affirmed in their competence and contribution, several psychological shifts occur:

- Stress hormones decrease
- Cognitive flexibility increases
- Motivation becomes intrinsic
- Engagement deepens
- Burnout risk drops

From a leadership perspective, this creates:

- Higher initiative
- Stronger buy-in
- Fewer power struggles
- Increased discretionary effort

Teachers begin doing more, not because they are forced, but because they are internally motivated.

This is the difference between compliance and commitment.

The Administrator's Role in Regulating Teacher Performance

Administrators often underestimate how powerfully their tone, timing, and presence affect teacher regulation.

For teachers, administrators function as:

- Authority figures

- Gatekeepers to security
- Evaluators of worth
- Symbols of safety or threat

Because of this, even small interactions carry significant nervous-system weight.

A regulated administrator provides:

- Predictability
- Emotional steadiness
- Fairness
- Respect
- Clarity

Teachers respond accordingly.

Why This Requires Administrators to Address Their Own Wounds

Here is the truth leadership programs rarely say aloud:

Administrators cannot provide safety they do not feel.

An administrator with unresolved trauma may:

- Withhold affirmation out of fear of losing authority
- Avoid vulnerability to protect identity
- Rely on control instead of trust
- Interpret teacher confidence as threat
- Struggle to celebrate others without comparison

None of this is intentional.

It is a nervous system trying to protect itself.

But when leaders heal their own wounds, several things change:

- Shared success no longer feels diminishing
- Teacher confidence no longer feels threatening
- Feedback becomes collaborative rather than corrective

This is not about becoming softer.
It is about becoming secure.

The Psychology Behind Why This Works

Several well-established psychological principles support this approach:

1. Self-Determination Theory

People perform best when three needs are met:

- Competence
- Autonomy
- Relatedness

Administrators who acknowledge teacher competence, allow professional autonomy, and build respectful relationships activate intrinsic motivation.

2. Polyvagal Theory

A calm, regulated leader signals safety.
Safety allows higher-order thinking, creativity, and collaboration.

Teachers mirror leadership regulation whether intentionally or not.

3. Social Learning Theory

People model behavior from those in power.
When administrators model respect, regulation, and confidence, teachers internalize those qualities.

What Teachers Need From Administrators (In Practice)

Teachers thrive when administrators:

- Acknowledge effort publicly and privately
- Separate mistakes from identity
- Give feedback without humiliation
- Protect teachers from unnecessary stress
- Trust professional judgment
- Celebrate progress, not just outcomes
- Address issues directly rather than through surveillance

These actions do not weaken authority.
They strengthen it.

The Outcome for Administrators

When administrators meet teachers' nervous-system needs:

- Resistance decreases
- Initiative increases
- Trust deepens
- Schools stabilize
- Leadership becomes sustainable

Administrators experience fewer conflicts not because teachers are controlled, but because teachers are invested.

Leadership is not about extracting performance.
It is about creating the conditions where performance emerges.

When teachers feel safe, valued, and capable, they give more than what is required.

Not because they have to.
Because they want to.

And that begins with a leader who has done the work to regulate themselves first.

Chapter 24

Is This Happening Now or Is This Memory?

Teaching the Nervous System to Tell the Difference

Healing does not begin with forgetting what happened.
It begins with learning how to recognize when the past is speaking louder than the present.

For teachers who have been harmed by leadership, the question that quietly changes everything is this:

Is this reaction coming from now or from then?

This is not a question of weakness.
It is a skill.

And like all skills, it can be taught.

Why This Question Matters

When trauma has been part of a teacher's professional experience, the nervous system learns to stay alert. It scans for danger automatically, often faster than conscious thought.

This means a current situation may activate a response that feels urgent, overwhelming, or disproportionate even when the present conditions are different.

Without this awareness, teachers often:

- Assume all leadership is dangerous
- Interpret neutral actions as threats
- React emotionally before gathering information
- Feel ashamed for being "too sensitive"

The question now or then interrupts this cycle.

It creates a pause.

What This Question Does and Does Not Mean

Asking, "Is this now or then?" does not mean:

- Ignoring instincts
- Gaslighting yourself
- Minimizing past harm
- Forcing trust where it doesn't belong

It means sorting information accurately.

Some environments are unsafe.
Some leaders do repeat harmful patterns.
And some fear belongs to an experience that has already happened.

Healing begins when teachers can tell the difference.

How Trauma Blurs Time

Trauma collapses time.

The body does not distinguish between:

- A current principal requesting a meeting
- And a past principal who used meetings to intimidate

The nervous system reacts as if both are the same.

This is why teachers may feel:

- Panic before an observation
- Dread opening emails

- A surge of anger or fear without clear cause

The body is responding to memory, not necessarily to reality.

Teaching the Difference: A Practical Framework

Teachers can begin differentiating now from then by walking through three deliberate steps.

Step 1: Name the Trigger

Ask:

- What specifically set off this reaction?
- Was it a tone, a phrase, a setting, or a reminder?

Example:

"This email reminded me of how my former principal used documentation against me."

Naming the trigger removes shame and adds clarity.

Step 2: Compare the Context

Ask:

- What is actually happening right now?
- What evidence do I have of threat in this moment?

Compare:

- Past leader's behavior vs. current leader's pattern
- One isolated action vs. repeated behavior
- Assumption vs. documented reality

This step grounds the teacher in facts, not fear.

Step 3: Decide, Don't React

Instead of reacting automatically, teachers regain choice.

They can ask:

- Do I need more information?
- Is a boundary required?
- Is this something to monitor rather than confront?
- Does this environment feel consistently unsafe or just unfamiliar?

This step restores agency.

When Fear Belongs to the Past

Sometimes teachers realize:

- The current leader is predictable
- Feedback is consistent and respectful
- There is no pattern of retaliation

In these cases, the fear is not a warning.
It is an echo.

Acknowledging this allows teachers to:

- Calm the nervous system
- Rebuild trust slowly
- Respond proportionally
- Stay present instead of bracing for impact

This is not denial.
It is healing.

When Fear Belongs to the Present

Other times, teachers recognize:

- Dismissal of concerns
- Patterned intimidation
- Lack of transparency
- Shifting expectations

In these cases, fear is information.

The goal is not to override it but to use it wisely:

- Document
- Seek support
- Establish boundaries
- Plan an exit if necessary

Awareness protects.

Why This Distinction Restores Power

Trauma removes choice.

Differentiation restores it.

When teachers can separate now from then, they stop living in constant reaction. They stop assuming every leader is dangerous and stop forcing themselves to tolerate environments that truly are.

They begin to trust themselves again.

You are not broken because your body remembers.
You are not weak because you hesitate.

Reclaiming Trust Slowly and On Your Terms

Trust does not return through forced positivity or "fresh starts."

It returns through:

- Consistent, predictable leadership behavior
- Transparency
- Follow-through
- Respect for boundaries
- Time

And sometimes, trust does not return in the same environment at all.

Leaving is not failure.
It is information.

If one experience with a principal or supervisor changed how you see the profession, you are not weak.

You were impacted.

Your vigilance is not a flaw.
It is evidence that something mattered.

Healing does not ask you to forget what happened.
It asks you to stop letting one person's misuse of power define your worth, your competence, or your future.

You are not paranoid.
You are responding to a system that once taught you it was not safe.

Chapter 25

Protecting Yourself While You Teach

Practical Tools for Staying Regulated, Grounded, and Whole

Understanding trauma changes how teachers see their experiences. But understanding alone is not enough.

Teachers also need ways to protect themselves in real time during meetings, observations, difficult emails, and long days that stretch the nervous system thin.

This chapter exists to bridge insight and action.
Not to harden you.
But to help you remain present without being consumed.

Why Insight Without Tools Can Feel Overwhelming

Many teachers reach awareness and then feel exposed.

They think:

- Now I see what's happening, but I still have to work here.
- I understand my triggers, but my body reacts anyway.
- I know I need boundaries, but I don't know how to hold them professionally.

This is not failure.
It is the moment where support must become practical.

Healing inside a system requires skills, not just clarity.

Tool #1: Grounding the Body at Work

Trauma lives in the nervous system, not in thought.
So regulation must include the body.

Simple grounding practices teachers can use discreetly:

- Place both feet flat on the floor and press gently for 10 seconds
- Take one slow inhale through the nose, exhale through the mouth twice as long
- Name silently: five things I see, three things I hear, one thing I feel

These techniques signal safety to the brain and reduce fight-or-flight responses without drawing attention.

Grounding is not weakness.
It is neurological first aid.

Tool #2: Preparing for Triggering Situations

Teachers often feel blindsided because trauma reduces predictability.

Preparation restores control.

Before meetings, observations, or conversations, ask:

- What is my role here?
- What is within my control?
- What outcome do I realistically need not hope for?

Set an internal anchor:

I can remain calm even if the other person does not.

This mental framing reduces emotional escalation and preserves dignity.

Tool #3: Neutral Professional Language

Trauma can silence or flood teachers emotionally.

Neutral language protects both professionalism and self-respect.

Examples:

- "I'd like clarification on expectations."
- "Can you share how this will be evaluated?"
- "I need time to process this before responding."
- "I'm open to feedback when it's specific and actionable."

This language is not defensive.
It is stabilizing.

Tool#4: Documentation Without Obsession

Documentation is not about paranoia.
It is about clarity.

Healthy documentation:

- Records dates, not interpretations
- Quotes exact language
- Focuses on patterns, not isolated moments

This practice creates internal safety even if it is never used.

You don't document because you expect harm.
You document because you respect yourself.

Tool #5: Boundary Setting Without Explanation

Teachers often feel compelled to justify boundaries.

You do not need to explain your limits to earn respect.

Boundaries can sound like:

- "I'm not available outside contract hours."
- "I'll follow up during scheduled time."
- "That doesn't work for me."

Boundaries stated calmly teach others how to treat you.

When the System Pushes Back

Not all systems welcome regulated, self-respecting teachers.

Teachers who set boundaries, document concerns, and speak with clarity often expect that professionalism will be respected. In healthy institutions, it is.

But in some environments, regulation and integrity expose instability within the system itself.

When boundaries are punished, clarity emerges.

At that point, the work shifts from adaptation to decision-making.

Staying becomes a choice.
Leaving becomes a choice.

Both require strength.

When Survival Mode Changes the Classroom

When educators are forced to operate in constant survival mode, the nervous system never fully settles.

A teacher may continue delivering lessons, grading work, and maintaining routines, but internally the body remains in a state of tension and vigilance.

Over time, that pressure begins to change how people respond.

Patience shortens.
Energy declines.
Reactions become sharper.

Students notice more than adults realize.

They observe tone.
They observe tension.
They observe how adults speak to them and to one another.

In some cases, a teacher who once entered the profession with compassion may begin speaking to students in ways that send a different message.

Harsh comments may slip out during moments of exhaustion.

Sometimes the frustration goes even further when words is use as weapon.

These moments do not mean the teacher is a bad person.

They often mean the teacher has been operating in survival mode for far too long.

But when words begin to wound students rather than guide them, it is an important signal.

If the environment has pushed a teacher to the point where their language is harming the very students they care about, something must change.

Sometimes the most responsible decision is not to endure the system indefinitely.

Sometimes the responsible decision is to step away from an environment that no longer allows the teacher to show up as the educator they intended to be.

When teachers are regulated, they respond rather than react. They create classrooms where mistakes can become learning opportunities rather than moments of shame.

But when teachers are trapped in survival mode, that instability can quietly trickle down to students.

The goal of education is not simply to keep classrooms running.

It is to create environments where students feel safe enough to learn.

The Hidden Cost to Teacher Health

Living in prolonged survival mode also affects the body.

When stress becomes chronic, the brain repeatedly activates the fight-or-flight system, releasing stress hormones such as cortisol. Over time this disrupts normal body functions.

Research shows that chronic stress can contribute to:

- High blood pressure and heart disease
- Weakened immune system functioning
- Increased inflammation in the body
- Anxiety, depression, and cognitive exhaustion

Teachers experiencing prolonged burnout often report:

- Chronic fatigue
- Sleep disruption
- Frequent illness
- Headaches and physical tension

These symptoms are not signs of weakness.

They are signals from a nervous system that has been asked to endure too much for too long.

Teaching should never require sacrificing one's physical or mental health.

If a system repeatedly prevents teachers from functioning in a healthy, regulated way, remaining in that environment indefinitely may not serve students as well as we hope.

Sometimes leaving is not about giving up.

Sometimes it is about refusing to participate in conditions that harm both teachers and children.

Teaching was never meant to cost you your nervous system.

And with the right tools and the right environment, it doesn't have to.

Chapter 26

Understanding the System: The Game Behind the Profession

How to Navigate Professional Dynamics Without Losing Your Integrity

There is a hidden curriculum in schools.

It is not in the standards.
It is not in the evaluation rubric.
It is not in the teacher handbook.

But it determines career stability.

That hidden curriculum is what people call "the game."

If you are a teacher who values truth, directness, logic, and fairness, the game may feel dishonest.

If you are neurodivergent, especially on the autism spectrum, the game may feel confusing, destabilizing, and unjust.

Because the game is not about being correct.

It is about navigating hierarchy.

This chapter will tell you exactly what the game is.

And exactly how to play it.

What the Game Is

The game is the unwritten set of social and political rules that govern how power operates in schools.

It is not about instruction.

It is about positioning.

The game governs:

- When you raise concerns
- How you raise concerns
- Who you raise concerns to
- How you phrase disagreement
- How you protect hierarchy
- How you protect yourself

The game exists because schools are hierarchical systems.

Hierarchy means:

- The superintendent protects the district.
- The principal protects the building.
- The supervisor protects curriculum.
- Teachers are expected to align.

When alignment appears threatened, the system responds.

Not always to correct truth.

But to stabilize structure.

That is the game.

The Two Systems You Must Understand

Every school operates in two systems at the same time.

System#1: The Performance System

This system rewards:

- Strong instruction
- Student growth

- Documentation
- Planning
- Compliance
- Parent communication

Most morally driven teachers excel here.

They believe:

"If I do my job well, I will be safe."

That belief works only in System One.

System#2: The Political Relational System

This system governs:

- Hierarchy protection
- Perception
- Timing
- Tone
- Alignment
- Loyalty
- Authority preservation

You can perform perfectly in System One and still struggle if you ignore System Two.

Doing well in only one system is not enough.

Why Neurodivergent Teachers Struggle With the Game

Teachers who are neurodivergent or on the autism spectrum (Level 1) often share these traits:

- Literal processing
- Strong moral reasoning
- Direct communication
- Low tolerance for inconsistency
- Deep commitment to fairness
- Discomfort with vague expectations
- Expectation that rules mean what they say

They may:

- Take "autonomy" literally.
- Assume clarity means stability.
- Expect standards to be applied consistently.
- Raise contradictions directly.

When hierarchy responds defensively, it feels like injustice.

But what is happening is this:

You were operating in System One logic.

The system responded in System Two logic.

That mismatch creates distress.

The game requires six skills.

1. Understand That Public Unity Is More Important Than Being Right

If you challenge a supervisor's directive publicly, even logically, it can be perceived as destabilizing.

Play the game by:

- Asking clarifying questions privately first.
- Never exposing leadership inconsistency in a group setting.
- Protecting authority even when you disagree.

Being correct does not override hierarchy.

2. Frame Concerns as Alignment, Not Contradiction

Instead of:

"This doesn't make sense."

Say:

"I want to make sure I'm fully aligned. Can you clarify how this connects to…"

Same concern.
Different positioning.

The game is about framing.

3. Choose Timing Carefully

Do not raise complex concerns:

- In emotionally charged meetings.
- In front of others.
- When authority feels threatened.

- Immediately after tension.

Private, calm timing reduces perceived threat.

4. Build Relational Capital Before Raising Tension

Influence requires deposits before withdrawals.

Relational capital looks like:

- Showing support publicly.
- Being solution-oriented.
- Participating in initiatives.
- Avoiding visible resistance.

Once you have capital, critique lands differently.

5. Separate Emotional Reaction From Professional Posture

You may feel:

- Frustrated.
- Misunderstood.
- Correct.

That is internal.

Your posture must remain:

- Calm.
- Neutral.
- Aligned.

Emotional expression in hierarchy is interpreted as instability.

Regulation is power.

6. Document Strategically, Not Emotionally

Document:

- Student support.
- Parent communication.
- Directives.
- Clarifications.

Do not use documentation to prove inconsistency.

Use documentation to protect yourself.

There is a difference.

What Playing the Game Is Not

It is not:

- Lying.
- Being fake.
- Betraying students.
- Abandoning integrity.

It is:

Understanding the environment in which integrity operates.

You can still advocate.

You must do it strategically.

Why Doing the Right Thing Isn't Always Enough

Many teachers believe:

"I told the truth. That should protect me."

In System One, yes.

In System Two, truth must be delivered with calibration.

Hierarchy does not reward exposure.

It rewards stability.

If your truth feels destabilizing, resistance may follow.

That does not mean you were wrong.

It means you ignored System Two.

How to Know You Are Struggling With the Game

You may notice:

- Repeated feelings of being misunderstood.
- Belief that others are irrational.
- Surprise when tension escalates.
- Emotional withdrawal after conflict.
- Moving schools frequently.
- Fear of targeting after disagreement.

These are not signs of incompetence.

They are signs of operating in one system only.

How to Navigating the Game Without Losing Yourself

1. Continue excelling in instruction.
2. Ask privately before challenging publicly.
3. Frame alignment language carefully.
4. Regulate emotional tone.

5. Observe patterns before reacting.
6. Protect relationships intentionally.
7. Do not equate disagreement with danger.

You can be principled and strategic at the same time.

Chapter 27

Your Integrity as a Teacher Still Matters

Choosing Dignity and Strength in a Profession That Tests Both

There comes a point often quietly when a teacher begins to wonder whether the work has changed them in ways that cannot be undone.

Not because the students are unlovable.
Not because the content has lost meaning.
But because carrying responsibility without safety takes a toll.

Many teachers reach this chapter feeling tired in a way rest does not fix. They question their instincts. They hesitate before speaking. They brace themselves where confidence once lived.

This chapter exists to say something clearly and without qualification:

What you have experienced has shaped you.
It has not erased you.

Being Changed Is Not the Same as Being Broken

Trauma does not leave teachers unchanged.
But change is not damaged.

After harmful experiences, many teachers become:

- More cautious
- More observant
- More deliberate with their energy
- Less willing to tolerate chaos disguised as "normal"

These are not losses.
They are adaptations.

Psychological research on post-traumatic growth shows that individuals often develop stronger boundaries, deeper empathy, and clearer values after adversity. The shift may feel like loss because innocence is gone, but clarity has taken its place.

You are not weaker because you see more clearly now.
You are wiser.

Dignity Is a Professional Right

Teaching has quietly normalized sacrifice.

Teachers are praised for:

- Working through illness
- Absorbing emotional labor
- Accepting disrespect as part of the job
- Enduring unsafe environments in the name of students

But dignity is not something to earn.
It is something you are entitled to.

You do not owe a system your health.
You do not owe leadership, your silence.
You do not owe a school your sense of self.

Remaining in education does not require self-erasure.

Redefining Strength

Strength in teaching has long been mis-defined as endurance.

Staying no matter the cost.
Absorbing harm without complaint.
Pushing through when the body signals stop.

That is not strength.
That is survival.

Real strength looks different:

- Knowing when to push and when to pause
- Setting boundaries without apology
- Choosing environments that support growth
- Protecting your nervous system so you can remain present

Strength does not require you to harden.
It requires you to remain whole.

You Can Stay Soft Without Staying Exposed

One of the deepest fears teachers carry after trauma is this:

I fear that in learning to protect myself; I will have to give up the tenderness that allows me to care.".

The opposite is true.

Boundaries preserve compassion.
Safety allows empathy to breathe.

When teachers stop overextending, they show up more fully for students. When they are not bracing for harm, they can listen, respond, and teach with clarity.

You do not have to choose between caring and protecting yourself.
You are allowed both.

Success Is No Longer External

For many teachers, success once meant:

- Approval from leadership
- Positive evaluations
- Being seen as dependable
- Being chosen, praised, or recognized

After trauma, those measures lose their power.

Success becomes internal:

- Am I aligned with my values?
- Do I feel safe enough to do my job well?
- Am I able to leave work without carrying it home?

This shift is not resignation.
It is maturity.

Staying Is a Choice. Leaving Is Also a Choice.

Some teachers will continue in the profession with renewed clarity. Others will step away to preserve their health and dignity.

Neither choice is a failure.

Leaving does not mean you couldn't handle it.
Staying does not mean you must tolerate harm.

What matters is that the decision is made consciously, not from fear, guilt, or pressure, but from self-respect.

What Was Not Taken From You

Trauma may have taken ease.
It may have taken innocence.
It may have taken trust.

But it did not take:

- Your skill
- Your insight
- Your impact
- Your ability to reach students
- Your worth

Those remain.

They always have.

If you are still here still teaching, still caring, still questioning there is strength in that.

Not the kind that burnt itself out.
The kind that endures because it is rooted in dignity.

You do not need to prove your value by suffering.
You do not need permission to protect yourself.

You are still a good teacher.

Hold Your Head High: The Strength and Dignity of Teaching

Hold Your Head High: The Work Matters, and So Do You**

There are moments in teaching when the weight feels heavier than expected.

You carry responsibility for students, expectations from leadership, pressure from systems, and the emotional demands of the classroom. Some days feel fulfilling. Other days feel invisible. And there are moments when it may seem as if the effort you give is not fully seen or understood.

Yet the work you do requires a level of strength and endurance that few professions demand.

Teaching calls for patience under pressure, emotional steadiness, intellectual focus, and the ability to remain composed even when situations feel challenging. Each day, you offer structure, consistency, and guidance to students who depend on your presence more than they may ever express.

This is not ordinary work.
It is meaningful, demanding work that shapes lives overtime.

Carry Yourself With Earned Confidence

You prepared for this profession.
You committed to it.
You continue to show up for it.

That matters.

When you walk into your school building, walk with quiet confidence in what you bring to the space. Your preparation, your dedication, and your consistency contribute to an environment where students can learn and grow.

Hold yourself with dignity.
Speak with clarity.
Carry yourself with the assurance that your work has purpose.

Professional confidence is not about recognition from others.
It comes from understanding the value of what you contribute each day.

Maintaining Perspective

There will be moments when the environment feels discouraging or when interactions feel difficult. In those moments, it is important to remember that teaching exists within complex systems shaped by many pressures and perspectives.

Not every challenge is a reflection of your ability.
Not every criticism defines your impact.
Not every difficult interaction tells the full story of your work.

Maintaining perspective allows you to continue forward with steadiness rather than discouragement.

Your role is to teach, guide, and support students with professionalism and care. When you remain grounded in that purpose, you protect both your effectiveness and your well-being.

Holding Yourself in Esteem

This profession requires an internal sense of worth.
While encouragement from others is valuable, the most sustainable confidence comes from within.

Recognize what you manage each day.
Acknowledge the effort required to remain patient, consistent, and focused.
Give yourself credit for the stability you provide in the lives of your students.

Hold yourself in high esteem because your work has meaning.
Walk into your classroom knowing that your presence matters.
Stand in the value of what you contribute.

A Closing Word of Hope

There is hope.

Somewhere, there is a superintendent, principal, or supervisor who sees your dedication and respects your approach to teaching. Leadership that values your professionalism and supports your growth does exist.

Do not let one difficult experience convince you otherwise.

Your place, a school where you can teach with clarity, breathe with ease, and work with integrity, is possible. It may come at a different time or in a different form than you first imagined, but it has not passed you by.

When discouragement feels heavy, return to what sustains you. For many, that includes faith and reflection. Returning to familiar words of comfort, such as those found in bible scriptures can remind you that you are not alone, even in demanding seasons.

You are seen.
You are supported.
And this moment is not the final chapter of your journey.

Continue forward with dignity.
Teach with purpose.
Hold onto hope.

The work you do still matters, and so do you

Chapter 28

A Teacher's Confession

For the Teacher Carrying This Quiet Guilt

There is a kind of guilt that many teachers carry but rarely speak about. The guilt of giving more to their students than to their own children.

The profession rarely talks about this part.

It celebrates dedication, sacrifice, and the emotional investment teachers make in their students. What it rarely acknowledges is the quiet internal conflict that follows many teachers home. It is the realization that the energy required to care for other people's children can leave less available for their own children.

There are also the moments the profession quietly takes from them in ways others may never notice. Back-to-School Night arrives, and they stand in front of other families explaining how they will care for their children throughout the year. Yet somewhere else, another teacher may glance at their own child's desk and notice it empty because no one was able to show up for their children that night.

And then comes the moment many teachers never admit out loud.

They realize that the compassion they offered generously throughout the day has limits by the time they reach home. By the end of the day when their children needs help with homework, they are exhausted in ways that are difficult to explain, not just physically, but also emotionally. The patience that felt natural in the classroom now requires effort. They sometimes respond with the very impatience they once vowed would never exist in their homes.

It is not the parent they intended to be.

It is the parent exhaustion created.

And the guilt that follows is heavy.

These moments accumulate quietly.

They live in the space between responsibility and love, between professional calling and parental presence.

For many teachers, this becomes a silent confession carried within them.

The guilt exists because the love exists.

And for many educators, understanding themselves, understanding the emotional cost of this work is part of learning how to hold both roles with greater awareness, compassion, and honesty. Their children always mattered.

If you recognize yourself in this confession, you are not alone. The first step is understanding an important truth: guilt does not mean failure. Often, it is simply evidence of how deeply you care.

Managing both roles begins with accepting that perfection is not possible in either one.

Some days you will show up fully for your students and still have energy left for your family. Other days the classroom will take more than you expected. What matters most is not that every moment is perfect, but that your children experience your love consistently over time.

Setting boundaries around work that follows you home can create space for your family. Not every paper needs to be graded that night. Not every email requires an immediate response. Protecting even small pockets of time for your own children can help restore balance.

Equally important is practicing repair. When exhaustion leads to impatience, acknowledging it matters. A simple conversation with your child admitting that you were tired and that they deserved better in that moment, teaches them something powerful: that relationships can recover and grow through honesty.

Your children do not need a perfect parent.

They need a parent who loves them, who tries again, and who continues to show up.

Finally, remember that the same compassion you offer your students deserves to be extended to yourself. Teachers are often the first to forgive mistakes in children and the last to forgive them in themselves.

Holding both roles, educator and parent will always involve tension. But it can also offer something unique: the opportunity for your children to witness the depth of your care for others and the strength it takes to serve a profession built on compassion.

And that, too, is a lesson they will carry with them.

References and Research Informing This Work

This work reflects the author's experience as an educator along with insights drawn from established research in psychology, trauma studies, and education. The following sources informed the perspectives discussed throughout this book.

Adverse Childhood Experiences (ACE) Study
Centers for Disease Control and Prevention (CDC). (2023).
Adverse Childhood Experiences (ACEs).
https://www.cdc.gov/violenceprevention/aces

Jennings, P. A. (2015).
Mindfulness for Teachers: Simple Skills for Peace and Productivity in the Classroom.
New York, NY: W. W. Norton & Company.

National Center for Education Statistics (NCES).
U.S. Department of Education.
Teacher Follow-Up Survey (TFS).

About the Author

Ingrid Fullerton is an educator with over 17 years of experience in public education, serving as a math teacher, math coach, and curriculum writer. Throughout her career, she has worked in a variety of school settings, including urban districts, suburban communities, and schools serving both affluent and economically challenged populations. These experiences have provided her with a broad perspective on how educational systems, community environments, and childhood experiences influence student development and learning.

She has worked extensively with multilingual learners and students performing below grade level, developing instructional approaches that emphasize conceptual understanding, equity, and student engagement.

In addition to her work in the classroom, Ingrid is the author of principal certification study guides designed to support educators preparing for school leadership examinations. Her writing often explores the intersection of education, childhood experiences, emotional development, and professional environments.

She is also the author of *The Awakening: Healing After Childhood Trauma and the Truth That a Child Cannot Stop Abuse* and *The Reclamation: Understanding and Healing the Wounds of* Abandonment.

The Journey Continues

The Awakening: Healing After Childhood Trauma and the Truth That a Child Cannot Stop Abuse

The Awakening explores a truth many survivors struggle to accept: a child cannot stop abuse when their safety and survival depend on the very adults responsible for their care. Through insight, reflection, and real-world understanding, this book helps readers untangle the burden of misplaced responsibility and begin the process of healing from childhood trauma.

The Reclamation: Understanding and Healing the Wounds of Abandonment

The Reclamation explores the many ways abandonment shapes a child's emotional world and the lasting impact it can have on identity, relationships, and trust.

Abandonment does not always appear as physical absence, it can take many forms, emotional withdrawal, inconsistency, neglect, or the quiet message that a child's needs do not matter.
This book helps readers recognize these patterns and begin the process of understanding and healing the wounds abandonment leaves behind.

www.ingramcontent.com/pod-product-compliance
Lightning Source LLC
LaVergne TN
LVHW010913110826
845149LV00013B/2350